INTRODUCING
ISSUES WITH
OPPOSING
VIEWPOINTS®

Islam

Lauri S. Scherer, *Book Editor*

GREENHAVEN PRESS
A part of Gale, Cengage Learning

GALE
CENGAGE Learning·

Detroit • New York • San Francisco • New Haven, Conn • Waterville, Maine • London

Elizabeth Des Chenes, *Director, Publishing Solutions*

For more information, contact:
Greenhaven Press
27500 Drake Rd.
Farmington Hills, MI 48331-3535
Or you can visit our Internet site at gale.cengage.com

Articles in Greenhaven Press anthologies are often edited for length to meet page requirements. In addition, original titles of these works are changed to clearly present the main thesis and to explicitly indicate the author's opinion. Every effort is made to ensure that Greenhaven Press accurately reflects the original intent of the authors. Every effort has been made to trace the owners of copyrighted material.

Cover image © Omer N. Raja/Shutterstock.com.

LIBRARY OF CONGRESS CATALOGING-IN-PUBLICATION DATA

Islam / Lauri S. Scherer, Book Editor.
    p. cm. -- (Introducing issues with opposing viewpoints)
Includes bibliographical references and index.
ISBN 978-0-7377-5682-1 (hardcover)
1. Islam--United States. 2. Islam. I. Scherer, Lauri S.
BP67.U6I84 2012
297--dc23
    2011051148

Printed in the United States of America
1 2 3 4 5 6 7 16 15 14 13 12

Contents

Chapter 3: What Is the Status of Islam and Muslims in the United States?

Foreword

Indulging in a wide spectrum of ideas, beliefs, and perspectives is a critical cornerstone of democracy. After all, it is often debates over differences of opinion, such as whether to legalize abortion, how to treat prisoners, or when to enact the death penalty, that shape our society and drive it forward. Such diversity of thought is frequently regarded as the hallmark of a healthy and civilized culture. As the Reverend Clifford Schutjer of the First Congregational Church in Mansfield, Ohio, declared in a 2001 sermon, "Surrounding oneself with only like-minded people, restricting what we listen to or read only to what we find agreeable is irresponsible. Refusing to entertain doubts once we make up our minds is a subtle but deadly form of arrogance." With this advice in mind, Introducing Issues with Opposing Viewpoints books aim to open readers' minds to the critically divergent views that comprise our world's most important debates.

Introducing Issues with Opposing Viewpoints simplifies for students the enormous and often overwhelming mass of material now available via print and electronic media. Collected in every volume is an array of opinions that captures the essence of a particular controversy or topic. Introducing Issues with Opposing Viewpoints books embody the spirit of nineteenth-century journalist Charles A. Dana's axiom: "Fight for your opinions, but do not believe that they contain the whole truth, or the only truth." Absorbing such contrasting opinions teaches students to analyze the strength of an argument and compare it to its opposition. From this process readers can inform and strengthen their own opinions, or be exposed to new information that will change their minds. Introducing Issues with Opposing Viewpoints is a mosaic of different voices. The authors are statesmen, pundits, academics, journalists, corporations, and ordinary people who have felt compelled to share their experiences and ideas in a public forum. Their words have been collected from newspapers, journals, books, speeches, interviews, and the Internet, the fastest growing body of opinionated material in the world.

Introducing Issues with Opposing Viewpoints shares many of the well-known features of its critically acclaimed parent series, Opposing Viewpoints. The articles are presented in a pro/con format, allowing readers to absorb divergent perspectives side by side. Active reading questions preface each viewpoint, requiring the student to approach the material thoughtfully and carefully. Useful charts, graphs, and cartoons supplement each article. A thorough introduction provides readers with crucial background on an issue. An annotated bibliography points the reader toward articles, books, and websites that contain additional information on the topic. An appendix of organizations to contact contains a wide variety of charities, nonprofit organizations, political groups, and private enterprises that each hold a position on the issue at hand. Finally, a comprehensive index allows readers to locate content quickly and efficiently.

Introducing Issues with Opposing Viewpoints is also significantly different from Opposing Viewpoints. As the series title implies, its presentation will help introduce students to the concept of opposing viewpoints and learn to use this material to aid in critical writing and debate. The series' four-color, accessible format makes the books attractive and inviting to readers of all levels. In addition, each viewpoint has been carefully edited to maximize a reader's understanding of the content. Short but thorough viewpoints capture the essence of an argument. A substantial, thought-provoking essay question placed at the end of each viewpoint asks the student to further investigate the issues raised in the viewpoint, compare and contrast two authors' arguments, or consider how one might go about forming an opinion on the topic at hand. Each viewpoint contains sidebars that include at-a-glance information and handy statistics. A Facts About section located in the back of the book further supplies students with relevant facts and figures.

Following in the tradition of the Opposing Viewpoints series, Greenhaven Press continues to provide readers with invaluable exposure to the controversial issues that shape our world. As John Stuart Mill once wrote: "The only way in which a human being can make some approach to knowing the whole of a subject is by hearing what can be said about it by persons of every variety of opinion and studying all modes in which it can be looked at by every character of mind. No wise man ever acquired his wisdom in any mode but this." It is to this principle that Introducing Issues with Opposing Viewpoints books are dedicated.

Introduction

In the twenty-first century, no other religion has faced the number or kind of criticisms, defenses, accusations, and inquiries as has Islam. The seemingly ongoing debates over whether Islam is a violent or peaceful religion, whether Islam respects or oppresses human rights, and whether Islam threatens or complements democracy are in part based on Islam's vast reach: It is not only the world's second-largest religion but is growing so rapidly that as of 2012, more than 1 in 5 people on the planet were Muslim. By 2030, if current trends continue, even more of the world's people will be believers of Islam: Work by the Pew Research Center shows that Islam will have grown so much over the next twenty years that more than 1 in 4 people on the planet—26.4 percent of the total population—will be Muslim. Indeed, the world's Muslim population is slated to increase by about 35 percent by that time, composing about 2.2 billion of the world's total projected population of 8.3 billion.

In addition to its explosive growth, Islam is also a lightning rod for discussion and debate because it has played a role, for better or worse, in many of the hot-button issues of the day: Culture, immigration, assimilation, women's issues, terrorism, and democracy, to name a few. In 2011 many of these issues were simultaneously thrust into the spotlight as several countries in the Middle East—largely Muslim and ruled by autocratic, repressive dictators—seemed reborn in a cacophony of democratic outpouring. From Tunisia to Egypt, mass protests resulted in the overthrow of brutal dictators Zine al-Abidine Ben Ali (of Tunisia), Hosni Mubarak (of Egypt), and Muammar Qaddafi (of Libya), all of whom for decades had ruled their people with an iron fist. Participating in what became known as the "Arab Spring," people of these countries poured into the streets, demanding freedom, justice, political representation, and other rights. In other countries, like Syria and Yemen, similar protests were attempted but quashed, with dictators like Bashar al-Assad (of Syria) and Ali Abdullah Saleh (of Yemen) keeping their grip on power.

The eruption of the Arab Spring, coupled with the Muslim population boom and high immigration rates to Western nations, raised the issue of whether Islam is inherently compatible with democracy—a frequently asked and difficult-to-answer question. Islam is an all-encompassing religion; it dictates every part of a believer's day, from what they can eat and wear, to what times they must pray. Islamic law—called sharia—trumps all other law, and in Islam, there is no such concept as separation of church and state, a principle at the very basis of government in the United States and other Western democracies.

These aspects of Islam have caused many to claim it to be inherently undemocratic. According to Middle East commentator and Islam expert Daniel Pipes, "To render Islam consistent with democratic ways will require profound changes in its interpretation." Pipes explains the ways in which sharia undermines democratic principles, eschews equal participation, and, above all, enforces the needs and beliefs of the collective over those of the individual: "Developed over a millennium ago, [sharia] presumes autocratic rulers and submissive subjects, emphasizes God's will over popular sovereignty, and encourages violent jihad to expand Islam's borders. Further, it anti-democratically privileges Muslims over non-Muslims, males over females, and free persons over slaves."[1] Pipes thinks it is impossible for Islam to serve as the basis for a democracy unless sharia is excised from it. This has worked in Turkey, for example, which functions as a democracy because it emphasizes the primary nature of secularism by banning certain public displays of religion, such as wearing head scarves in government buildings or displaying signs in Arabic.

If Islam must carve from itself the very system of law that makes it operate, however, one must wonder whether that relationship with democracy is possible at all. These are the thoughts of journalist Jeanette Windle, who thinks it is impossible for Islam to coexist with democracy. "Yes, of course, [such coexistence is possible] if democracy is defined simply as holding elections for a chosen slate of local politicians," she writes. "A resounding 'no' if one's definition of democracy includes any semblance of human rights and freedom."[2] Windle points out that sharia prohibits criticizing Islam (and thus denies free speech), forces nonbelievers to adhere to Islamic dietary and cultural rules, prescribes death for Muslims who convert from the religion, and assigns different values, rights, and responsibilities to men and women (in some Muslim countries that adhere strictly to sharia, a woman's testimony is worth less than a man's in court, for example; in others, women have been jailed or sentenced to death for the crime of adultery).

And yet, Islam has proven its compatibility with democracy in several significant ways. With so many Muslims on the planet, devotees of Islam are incredibly diverse: They speak dozens of languages, live in hundreds of countries, and ascribe to myriad cultural and ethnic practices. Such diversity lends itself very well to democracy, it is argued. Islam coexists with democracy in practice, too: Indonesia, the world's largest Muslim country, is also a democracy.

Furthermore, Muslims living in nondemocratic countries report high respect for the institution of democracy: A Pew Research Center poll taken after the Egyptian revolution in 2011, for example, found that 59 percent of Muslims in Egypt said that democracy was preferable to any other kind of government. Similar polls have uncovered overwhelming support and admiration for democracy in the Muslim nations of Jordan, Morocco, and Algeria. In the United States, millions of Muslims have assimilated easily and eagerly, with a 2011 Pew Research Center poll showing that 93 percent of Muslim Americans say they are primarily loyal to the United States.

Where Islam does not coexist with democracy, it has been explained that the religion has been co-opted by corrupt Muslim leaders and become a tool for exploitation and oppression. Iranian human rights activist Shirin Ebadi is just one person who points out that these leaders have deviated from the core tenets of Islam, which she says is inherently committed to democracy, rights, justice, and equality. For example, Ebadi points out that the Prophet Muhammad allowed both Muslims and non-Muslims to live freely in the Islamic world, showing dedication to freedom of religion, a key tenet of democracy. "Lack of democratization in the Islamic world does not emanate from the essence of Islam," writes Ebadi. "Rather, it is due to the unwillingness for numerous reasons of Islamic states to embrace an interpretation of Islam that is compatible with human rights, preserves individual and social freedoms, and advocates democratic statecraft."[3] Ebadi and others argue that Muslim nations that are autocratic or despotic are that way because of Arab tribal history, not because of Islam.

It remains to be seen whether Islam can coexist with democracy in all environments and whether the Arab Spring will ultimately result in a region of stable, Islamic democracies. These are among the many topics covered in *Introducing Issues with Opposing Viewpoints: Islam.* Students will also consider opposing arguments on how women are treated in Islam, whether Islam condones honor killings, if American Muslims are discriminated against, and how states should react to proposals to ban sharia. Guided reading questions and essay prompts help readers articulate their own opinions on this sensitive, complex, and multifaceted topic.

Notes

1. Daniel Pipes, "Is Islam Compatible with Democracy?," *FrontPage Magazine,* April 15, 2008. http://archive.frontpagemag.com/read Article.aspx?ARTID=30611.
2. Jeanette Windle, "Is Democracy Enough?," January 10, 2009. http://jeanettewindle.blogspot.com/2009/01/is-democracy -enough.html.
3. Shirin Ebadi, "Islam, Democracy, and Human Rights: Dr. Shirin Ebadi's Address at Syracuse University, May 10, 2004," *Orangebytes,* vol. 2, May 2004.

Chapter 1

Why Is Islam Linked to Terrorism?

There are over a billion people in the world who practice Islam. But some non-Muslims think it is a religion that thrives on violence.

Islam Produces and Inspires Terrorists

Amil Imani

"Truth be told, violence is the animating force of Islam."

In the following viewpoint Amil Imani argues that Islam is a violent religion that breeds violent followers. He explains that the Koran, or Qur'an, the Muslim holy book, contains many passages that inspire violence, murder, and domination. He also says that several people who were key founders of Islam were honored for acts of mass violence, which Imani says embedded violent values into the religion from its birth. Imani argues that violence is woven deeply into the fabric of Islam and concludes that Islam inspires its believers to commit acts of violence, murder, and destruction.

Imani is an Iranian American novelist, essayist, literary translator, public speaker, and political analyst.

AS YOU READ, CONSIDER THE FOLLOWING QUESTIONS:
1. According to Imani, what did Major Nidal Malik Hasan do on the morning of his fatal attack on Fort Hood?
2. What is the text of Quran 9:38, as cited by the author?
3. Who is Ali, as described by Imani?

There is a division of the house. On one side are the politically correct in government, the leftist mainstream media, and a raft of Islamist apologists. One and all are tripping over each other in reassuring us the mass murderers such as Maj. Nidal Malik Hasan[1] and suicide-bombers who detonate their explosive vests in crowded marketplaces and even mosques are individual anomalies and Islam is not responsible for what they do.

On the other side are those fed up with the innumerable daily horrific acts throughout the world that are clearly committed under the banner of Islam. In all fairness, there needs to be a distinction. Numerous criminal acts are also committed on a daily basis by non-Muslims. The critical difference is that non-Muslim criminals do not hoist a religious banner to justify their misdeeds, while the Muslims proudly claim that they commit their heinous acts in obedience to the dictates of their religious faith.

Islam Was Hasan's Inspiration

Would someone please explain what motivated Nidal Hasan, who at taxpayers' expense was educated from college all the way through medical school and post-medical-school training, to turn his deadly weapons against the nation that gave him everything he had?

If Islam had nothing to do with what Maj. Nidal Malik Hasan did, then why:

- did he repeatedly preach the ascendancy of Islam over the U.S. Constitution?
- did he publicly support Islamic suicide-bombing?
- did he proclaim his highest loyalty to Islam?
- was he in contact with violent anti-U.S. Islamists and a virulent Yemeni Imam [Muslim leader]?
- did he distribute copies of the Quran to people the morning of his bloody attack?
- did he keep screaming "Allahu akbar" [Allah (God) is great] as he heartlessly sprayed over a hundred bullets, killing thirteen and injuring some thirty innocent men and women?

---

1. Hasan is an American Muslim army major who on November 5, 2009, opened fire on his fellow soldiers at Fort Hood army base near Killeen, Texas, killing thirteen people and wounding dozens.

Islam Is the Culprit

Here is the truth, as bitter as it may be: Islam is the culprit. Islam is anything but a religion of peace. Violence is at the very core of Islam. Violence is institutionalized in the Muslims' holy book, the Quran, in many suras [chapters]:

> Quran 9:5 "Fight and kill the disbelievers wherever you find them, take them captive, harass them, lie in wait and ambush them using every stratagem of war."

> 9:112 "The Believers fight in Allah's cause; they slay and are slain, kill and are killed."

> 8:39 "So fight them until there is no more Fitnah (disbelief [non-Muslims]) and all submit to the religion of Allah alone (in the whole world)."

> 8:65 "O Prophet, urge the faithful to fight. If there are twenty among you with determination they will vanquish two hundred; if there are a hundred then they will slaughter a thousand unbelievers, for the infidels are a people devoid of understanding."

> 9:38 "Believers, what is the matter with you, that when you are asked to go forth and fight in Allah's Cause you cling to the earth? Do you prefer the life of this world to the Hereafter? Unless you go forth, He will afflict and punish you with a painful doom, and put others in your place."

> 47:4 "When you clash with the unbelieving Infidels in battle (fighting Jihad [holy battle] in Allah's Cause), smite their necks until you overpower them, killing and wounding many of them. At length, when you have thoroughly subdued them, bind them firmly, making (them) captives. Thereafter either generosity or ransom (them based upon what benefits Islam) until the war lays down its burdens. Thus are you commanded by Allah to continue carrying out Jihad against the unbelieving infidels until they submit to Islam."

And the Quran is considered by Muslims to be the word-for-word literal edicts of their god, Allah.

Shouting radical Islamic rhetoric, US Army major Nidal Malik Hasan (pictured) opened fire at Fort Hood, Texas, killing thirteen people and wounding dozens more.

Islam Promotes Intolerance, Hatred, Discrimination, and More

Right from the start, violence served as the engine of Islam under the command and supervision of Muhammad himself. For one, the Prophet's son-in-law cousin, Ali, was titled the Commander of the Faithful for his unsurpassed feats of butchery. With the assistance of one or two of his thugs, Ali beheaded some seven hundred captives, most of them Jews, in only one day. This man, highly esteemed by the prophet of Allah, carried a sword that had its own name—Zolfaghar. Ali's portrait, holding the menacing sword, adorns the homes and shops throughout Shiite[2] lands. And Ali is revered by the Shiites at the same level as Muhammad.

On the Sunni[3] side, Muhammad's co-revered is Umar, another unabashed killer of untold numbers. And of course, the choice weapon of these champions of the religion of peace was the sword. To this day, a sword adorns the flag of Saudi Arabia, the birthplace of the religion of peace.

2. Shiites are Islam's second-largest denomination and believe Ali was chosen by God to succeed Muhammad as head of Islam.
3. Sunnis form the largest Muslim denomination and accept Umar as the rightful heir of Muhammad as head of Islam.

And Islam, by the very nature of its doctrine, appeals to man's base nature. It promotes intolerance, hatred, discrimination, and much more: Quran 61:2: "O Muslims, why say one thing and do another? Grievously odious and hateful is it in the sight of Allah that you say that which you do not. Truly Allah loves those who fight in His Cause in a battle array, as if they were a solid cemented structure."

Like a Deadly, Contagious Disease

In reality, Islam is like a deadly, contagious disease. Once it invades the mind of its victim, it is capable of transforming him to a helpless pawn that has no choice but to execute what he is directed to do.

Of the reported 1.3 billion Muslims in the world, millions are already trapped in the terminal stages of this affliction, while millions of others are rapidly joining them. The people enslaved with the extreme cases of Islamic mental disease are highly infectious. They actively work to transmit the disease to others, while they themselves engage in horrific acts of mayhem and violence to demonstrate their unconditional obedience to the dictates of the Islamic cult.

The savagery and variety of the actions of these Islamic captives are seen daily around the globe. Many of these acts, committed under the banner of Islam, have become so commonplace that the world has come to view them as part and parcel of a troubled humanity. And, from time to time, the world is shocked into a passing and momentary realization of the evil deeds these Islamist robots commit. However, people quickly get over it, and they do nothing to seriously address this affliction.

> ## FAST FACT
>
> A March 2011 poll by the Pew Research Center found that 40 percent of Americans thought Islam was more likely than other religions to incite violence; 66 percent of conservative Republicans thought this.

The Dogma of Hate

The recent and dastardly mass murder at Fort Hood, committed by Maj. Nidal Malik Hasan, will be forgotten by the public before long.

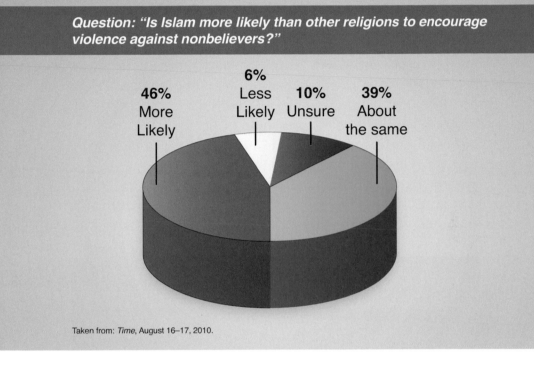

Islam Inspires Violence

A 2010 poll taken by *Time* found the majority of Americans think Islam is more likely than other religions to be a source or inspiration of violence.

Question: "Is Islam more likely than other religions to encourage violence against nonbelievers?"

46% More Likely

6% Less Likely

10% Unsure

39% About the same

Taken from: *Time*, August 16–17, 2010.

Life will continue on its deadly course, pushed along in a variety of ways by Islamists, the agents of death. Only the families who lost their loved ones and those who survived the bullets have to live the rest of their lives with incapacitating injuries. They likely won't be able to put the episode behind them.

The mass-murderer Hasan did not riddle people with bullets under the pressure of momentary insanity. The insanity—ironic in a man who was trained to help people with sanity—was introduced in him from the moment of birth and from the very early years when he prostrated himself five times daily toward Mecca in expression of total submission to the dogma of hate called Islam.

A true Muslim does not and cannot believe in freedom of choice. In the religion of Islam—"submission" [the meaning of the word

Islam]—everything is up to Allah, as clearly and repeatedly stipulated in the Quran. The *raison d'être* for the Muslim is unconditional submission to the will and dictates of Allah. Everything that a "good" Muslim does is contingent upon the will and decree of Allah, in which the Muslim is indoctrinated to believe.

Violence Is the Essence of Islam

Humanity is facing a deeply troubling dilemma. On the one hand is the desire of enlightened people to forge a diverse world into one society ruled by peace and justice, while on the other hand, Islamists are hellbent on imposing their stone-age system on everyone. Tellingly, the Muslims themselves are at one another's throats regarding which of dozens of Islamic sects' dogma should rule.

For now, Islam is busy with what it did from the time of its birth: fighting the non-Muslims, and infighting.

Truth be told, violence is the animating force of Islam. Islam is a religion born through violence, raised by violence, which thrives on violence, and which dies without violence.

EVALUATING THE AUTHORS' ARGUMENTS:

To make his argument, Amil Imani quotes several passages from the Koran that encourage violence, and even murder. What do you think Zeba Khan, author of the following viewpoint, might have to say about these passages? Sum up what you think Khan's perspective might be, and then state with which author you ultimately agree about whether the Koran encourages violence.

Islam Does Not Produce and Inspire Terrorists

Zeba Khan

> *"We must remember that the violent minority of a minority are motivated by politics, not religion."*

Islam is a peaceful, tolerant, and thoughtful religion that neither produces or inspires terrorists, argues Zeba Khan in the following viewpoint. She describes her own Muslim upbringing, which she remembers as serene and charitable. Khan says there are millions of Muslims just like her—people who value helping others, spreading love and justice, and opposing tyranny and oppression. Khan argues that every religion has some people who act violently and commit crime. With more than a billion followers in dozens of nations, Islam is bound to have a few people who go against their faith, she argues. Khan concludes that violence committed in Islam's name is not a reflection of the religion but rather of politically motivated individuals who have gone wrong. Her remarks come from a transcript of a debate held in New York City on whether Islam is a religion of peace. Afterward, the audience was supposed to vote on that topic.

Khan is a writer and advocate for Muslim American civic engagement.

AS YOU READ, CONSIDER THE FOLLOWING QUESTIONS:
  1. According to Khan, how many Muslims live in how many different countries?
  2. Who is Zainab Salbi, as mentioned by the author?
  3. Who is Mohammad Hamdani, as described by Khan?

I am a Muslim American woman born and raised in Toledo, Ohio, by two very loving Indian Muslim parents. My sister, brother, and I were raised in a middle-class American home. We went to Mosque on Sundays, attended Sunday school classes, and prayed the community prayer with our community of Pakistanis, Lebanese, and Syrian Muslims. When I was in high school, our Mosque president was a woman, who did not wear a headscarf. And it may come as a surprise to some of you, but for the entirety of my life men and women have prayed side by side at our Mosque, and both can enter the prayer hall using the same door.

A Respectful Muslim Upbringing

My parents are both very religious people, but they express their faith in different ways. My father emphasizes the devotional, and he tends to spend his time praying and reciting the Koran, whereas my mother emphasizes the more constructive approach.

She uses community service and volunteering to express hers. But what they both share is fundamental Islamic principles. First and foremost, seek knowledge. They urged their children, all three of us, to question, to have critical minds, and to doubt. They wanted us to engage fully with our faith and to question everything. They lived out the Koranic commandments that there is no compulsion in religion, and also that God said, in the Koran, "I made you into many tribes so that you might know one another." And as such, they enrolled me and my siblings in a Hebrew day school for nine years, where we learned Hebrew, read the Torah, and prayed in a synagogue almost every morning. They always wanted us to learn about other faiths, and they always made sure that we knew the difference, though, between Islam and Judaism. But they also made sure we also respected our Jewish sisters and brothers in faith.

My story is just one of 1.5 billion stories in some 57 countries. The Muslim population is one of the most diverse and eclectic in the world. We are Sunnis, we are Shias, and even in the Shia tradition there are Zaidis, Ismailis, Ismasheries [spelled phonetically from a transcript]. There are numerous madhhabs, or schools of thought, and Sufi mystic orders. Like Christians and Jews, Muslims can be observant, nonobservant, performist, humanist, secularist, extremist, mainstream, and there are even some Muslims who consider themselves culturally Muslims but are actually atheists.

The Vast Majority of Muslims Are Peaceful

Now, the motion before you tonight is asking you to determine whether Islam is a religion of peace. And at first blush, that might seem a bit tricky to decide. After all, the Koran and the Hadith have verses in them that point to peace and justice and love. But there are

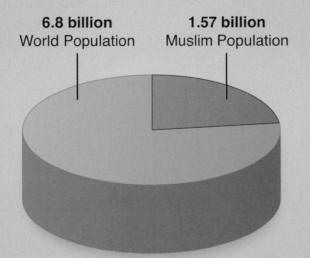

Nearly One in Four People on Earth Are Muslim

With more than 20 percent of the planet's population identifying with Islam, many argue that the vast majority of Muslims are peaceful.

6.8 billion
World Population

1.57 billion
Muslim Population

Taken from: Pew Research Center's Forum on Religion & Public Life. *Mapping the Global Population, October 2009.*

other verses that are violent, are about violence and about violence against specific people. So how then do we reconcile these seemingly contradictory verses? How then do we decide whether Islam is a religion of peace? The only way to answer that question is to take an honest look at the people who practice the faith and how they interpret it. According to Gallup's ground breaking study on what a billion Muslims think, 93 percent of Muslims around the world are peaceful, mainstream Muslims. Seven percent are what Gallup determines as politically radicalized. And within that seven percent, there's a smaller percent that has succumbed to the use of violence. Any percent is too much. But we must remember that the violent minority of a minority are motivated by politics, not religion. As Gallup concluded, what distinguishes the politically radicalized Muslims from the mainstream Muslims is their politics, not their piety. Robert Pape, a University of Chicago political scientist, further confirmed this in his book, *Dying to Win*, in which he came to the same conclusion, that the actions of terrorists are politically motivated, not through religion. The [Sri Lankan terrorist group the] Tamil Tigers, for example, which are predominantly a Hindu group, used and pioneered the use of suicide bombing, [and] did so for secessionist reasons, not for religious goals.

Violence Does Not Belong to Any Religion

Our opponents would have you believe that there is a take all, no winner clash between Islam and the West, and that Muslims who try to balance their Western values and Islam arrive at a state of cognitive dissonance and are left either mute or crazy by this internal struggle.

That description doesn't resonate for me or for my family or for my friends or for my community, because those two aspects of our identity were never in conflict with each other and were never introduced to us as in conflict with each other. I didn't realize that there were people out there who wondered whether people—Muslims like me—existed or could exist until after 9/11.

Loving, Peaceful People

Let me be clear. There are some horrifically violent criminals out there who twist our faith to justify their hate and their violence. But I am here to tell you they don't speak for Islam. Mohammad Hamdani [spelled phonetically], a first responder who died on 9/11, speaks for Islam. Hassan Askari, a Brooklyn Muslim who stepped in on the subway and saved a complete stranger who was being physically attacked because he was Jewish, he speaks for Islam. Zainab Salbi, through her organization Women for Women International, has assisted over a quarter of a million women across the world. She speaks for Islam. And the entire Muslim community of India, who, when the authorities asked them to take the militants who attacked Mumbai in 2008, said resoundingly and collectively no. We will not let the terrorists be buried with us.

Zainab Salbi (pictured) is the founder of Women for Women International, which has assisted thousands of women worldwide affected by war.

The media and those who profit from the narrative of Islam versus the West are never going to tell you my story or the stories of these Muslims who constitute the vast majority of Muslims around the world. But just because you may not hear us, it doesn't mean we're not speaking out. And just because you may not see us on TV, it doesn't mean we don't exist.

EVALUATING THE AUTHORS' ARGUMENTS:

Zeba Khan and Amil Imani, author of the previous viewpoint, both come from Islamic backgrounds. Yet they hold very different opinions on whether Islam inspires terrorists. Does it surprise you that two people from similar backgrounds would hold such opposing beliefs about their own faith? Why or why not? With which author do you ultimately agree about the nature of Islam? Quote from the text you found most convincing.

The United States Unfairly Links Muslims with Terrorism

"Accusations against American Muslims . . . that they have been uncooperative with law enforcement officials in preventing terrorism plots . . . amount to shameful bigotry."

Zareena Grewal

Zareena Grewal is an assistant professor of American Studies and Religious Studies at Yale University and director of the Center for the Study of American Muslims at the Institute for Social Policy and Understanding. In the following viewpoint she argues that Muslim Americans are unfairly linked to terrorism. She explains that the vast majority of American Muslims and Arabs love their country, shun extremist views, and publicly condemn terrorism. They have helped law enforcement capture suspected terrorists and have been instrumental in thwarting terrorist plots. Yet, says Grewal, Muslim Americans are discriminated against and viewed with suspicion by their fellow citizens and government representatives.

They are unfairly singled out to participate in Congressional hearings on terrorism. America has become rife with anti-Muslim sentiment, which in Grewal's opinion is unfair and undeserved. She warns that linking Muslims to terrorism is not only wrong but counterproductive because such treatment could turn patriotic Muslim Americans against their country.

AS YOU READ, CONSIDER THE FOLLOWING QUESTIONS:
1. How many terrorist plots does Grewal say Muslim Americans have helped to thwart?
2. What did a survey of mosques conducted by the Institute for Social Policy and Understanding find about the views of American Muslims, according to the author?
3. What does Grewal say are two of the very rare traits shared by Muslim terrorists and Muslims worldwide?

Representative Peter King (R) of New York is holding congressional hearings on the "threat of homegrown Islamic terrorism" today [March 10, 2011]. Mr. King has lodged a number of accusations against American Muslims, alleging that they have been uncooperative with law enforcement officials in preventing terrorism plots here in the United States. His accusations, however, are built on distortions of the facts that have been refuted by top law enforcement officials. The problem with the King hearings is not simply that they amount to shameful bigotry; these hearings are counterproductive. They fail to address the root causes of homegrown terrorism and alienate rather than engage one of the greatest assets in the fight against Islamic extremism—American Muslims.

American Muslims Love Their Country

As Attorney General Eric Holder stated recently, "The cooperation of Muslim and Arab-American communities has been absolutely essential in identifying, and preventing, terrorist threats." According to the Triangle Center on Terrorism and Homeland Security, Muslim American cooperation led to thwarted terrorist plots in 48 of 120 cases involving Muslim Americans. Last year, the RAND corporation reported that the low rate of would-be violent extremists indicates that American Muslims are opposed to "jihadist ideology and its exhortations to violence" and therefore, "a mistrust of American Muslims by other Americans seems misplaced."

Since 9/11, millions of research dollars have been spent on understanding American Muslims: how many there are, how religious they are, and how satisfied or "happy" they are living in the US. A 2007 Pew study, reassuringly titled "Muslim Americans: Mostly Middle Class and Mainstream," found them to be largely assimilated, politically moderate, and similar to other American religious groups in their values, degree of religious observance, and, yes, even happiness.

Muslim Americans Are Moderate and Mainstream

In a Duke University study, counterterrorism researchers found very low numbers of what they termed "radicalized" American Muslims and that American mosques were taking pragmatic steps to counter extremism. Some of these community-based initiatives include public and collective denunciations of terrorism, self-policing, developing community resources, and nurturing civic engagement.

In the face of this research, King still insists that 85 percent of American mosques have "extremist leadership" and that ordinary American Muslims are not opposed to terrorism. But a 2004 survey of mosque congregations in greater Detroit conducted by the Institute

US attorney general Eric Holder (pictured) has said that cooperation from Muslim and Arab American communities has been a key component in identifying potential terrorist threats.

for Social Policy and Understanding found that the vast majority of mosque participants shun extremist views (92 percent) and are virtually unanimous (93 percent) in supporting community service and political involvement.

Muslims Also Worry About Extremism

While studies show that most Muslim Americans shun extremism, King might ask: What about the remaining outliers who don't? What are we doing about them? Even if they only make up a tiny percentage of American Muslim communities, the scale of their violent destruction could be incalculable.

American Muslims are painfully aware of the fact that the actions of a few can have global, deleterious consequences on our society in general, and on Muslim communities in particular. That's why Muslim leaders are educating their youth, cooperating with law enforcement, and, repeatedly, publicly condemning terrorism. King and others concerned about homegrown terrorism ought to support them. Instead, King's hearings treat all Muslim Americans as dangerous outsiders, which undermines the counter-terrorism efforts within American mosques.

> **FAST FACT**
>
> An August 2011 Gallup poll found that nine out of ten Muslim Americans do not sympathize with the terrorist group al Qaeda. Also, 69 percent of American Muslims identify either very strongly or extremely strongly with the United States.

American Muslims Have Become Targets

While both the [George W.] Bush and [Barack] Obama administrations have gone to great lengths to defend Muslim Americans as patriotic citizens, 9/11 re-legitimized the once-discredited practice of racial profiling. In the 1990s, racial profiling had largely been dismissed as an inefficient, ineffective, and unfair policy that George W. Bush had openly condemned. But after 9/11, there was a new public consensus that racial profiling was essential for the nation's survival.

The Government Should Not Single Out Muslims

In 2011 Republican congressman Peter King, chair of the House Committee on Homeland Security, held hearings to explore radicalization among Muslim Americans. The majority of Americans thought that antiterrorism hearings should focus not just on Muslim Americans, but on religious extremism in whatever community it may exist.

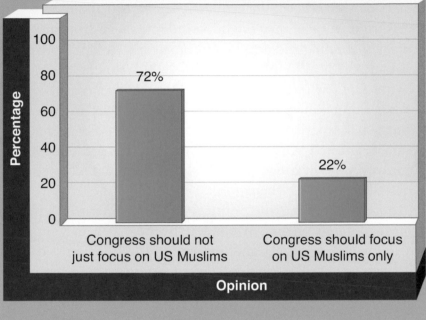

Taken from: PRRI/RNS Religion News Survey, February 2011.

In the wake of 9/11, Gallup polls found that one-third of New Yorkers supported the internment of Arab Americans and that even the majority of African Americans surveyed (71 percent) supported the racial profiling of Arabs. A 2006 Gallup poll showed that 39 percent of Americans believe all Muslims, even US citizens, should be forced to carry special identification cards.

Clearly, such anti-Muslim sentiments have not abated over time, evinced by the grass-roots opposition to the so-called "Ground Zero Mosque" in 2010. The protests devolved into a campaign against mosques throughout the country, in red states and blue states, in cities and small towns. Recently, more than a dozen states have introduced or approved measures to "ban sharia." Republican Tennessee state Senator Bill Ketron claims his proposed "sharia ban" is "a powerful counter-terrorism tool." However, the language of his bill is so sweeping and so misguided about what *sharia* is and is not, that, if passed, it would essentially make it a felony to be a devout Muslim in Tennessee.

Anti-Muslim Is Counterproductive

If King and other officials are genuinely concerned about preventing homegrown terrorism, they might consider the anti-Muslim climate they are perpetuating and do a bit of homework. Recent reports from the CIA and the NYPD [New York Police Department] indicate that two of the very few traits that Muslim "homegrown terrorists" share is a sense of moral outrage over the suffering of Muslims worldwide and a personal experience of discrimination and social alienation. If there are disaffected Muslim American youth who are susceptible to extremism, King's hearings and the "sharia bans" are likely to aggravate, not alleviate, their alienation.

Furthermore, this hostile political climate undermines Muslim community-based efforts to combat homegrown extremism by diverting precious energies and resources away from intra-community challenges toward shielding against external pressures, such as Islamophobic hearings and legislation.

Peace and Justice Will Beat Bigotry

Recently, the Muslim Public Affairs Council produced a counter-terrorism YouTube video featuring the who's who of American imams [Muslim prayer leaders] condemning terrorism and absolving Islam of any association with it. The video, "Injustice Cannot Defeat Injustice," has a reasonable message, but an apolitical tone. Although it purports to be addressing disaffected Muslim youth, the video's real audience seems to be non-Muslims. American Muslims have upheld their responsibility to combat extremism, but they need to take the political grievances of disaffected youth more seriously.

Ultimately, the most powerful counterterrorism strategy has come not from Capitol Hill but from Tahrir Square in Cairo, Egypt. The peaceful protests in the Middle East have demonstrated that global Muslim suffering is real and that its source is political, not religious. More important, those demonstrations prove that Muslim youth in the Middle East—and the US—can work for social justice and civil rights successfully, like American minorities before them, armed with patience and courage, rather than weapons.

EVALUATING THE AUTHOR'S ARGUMENTS:

Zareena Grewal uses numerous facts and statistics to make her argument that Muslims are unfairly linked to terrorism. Make a list of all the facts and statistics cited in her viewpoint, along with their source. Then, pair them with the idea they support. Which of these facts did you find most convincing, and why? Which of these facts did you find least convincing, and why?

Viewpoint 4

The United States Is Right to Link Muslims with Terrorism

Ralph Peters

"Muslim terrorist wannabes are busted again and again. And we're assured that 'Islam's a religion of peace.'"

In the following viewpoint Ralph Peters argues that Americans are right to link Muslims with terrorism, because, in his opinion, Muslims commit numerous acts of terrorism and do so while invoking their religion. As evidence, he adduces the case of Major Nidal Malik Hasan, a US Army major who in 2009 killed thirteen people and wounded dozens in a shooting spree at Fort Hood army base in Texas. Peters reports that Hasan was a devout Muslim who praised suicide bombers, posted anti-American hate speech on the Internet, and shouted Arabic phrases while he killed. In Peters's opinion, it is wrong to divorce Hasan's religion from his act of terrorism. Hasan invoked his religion and used it as his inspiration to kill, asserts Peters, and Americans should not pretend otherwise. Peters argues that Americans are too politically correct when it comes to dealing with the issue of Islam and terror.

Reluctant to be labeled as racist, Americans have refused to blame terrorist attacks on Islam, but Peters says they cannot ignore the truth behind most terrorist attacks. Denying the Islamic elements of terrorist acts will only put more Americans at risk, he concludes.

Peters is a retired US Army lieutenant colonel and a columnist for the *New York Post*.

AS YOU READ, CONSIDER THE FOLLOWING QUESTIONS:
1. Who, in the author's view, are cowards, and why?
2. In addition to the shooter what does Peters say is also to blame for the deaths at Fort Hood?
3. What does the author say happened in Kuwait in 2003?

On [November 5, 2009], a radicalized Muslim US Army officer shouting "Allahu Akbar!" [Allah is great!] committed the worst act of terror on American soil since 9/11. And no one wants to call it an act of terror or associate it with Islam.

What cowards we are. Political correctness [PC] killed those patriotic Americans at Ft. Hood as surely as the Islamist gunman did. And the media treat it like a case of non-denominational shoplifting.

A *Terrorist* Act

This was a terrorist act. When an extremist plans and executes a murderous plot against our unarmed soldiers to protest our efforts to counter Islamist fanatics, it's an act of terror. Period.

When the terrorist posts anti-American hate-speech on the Web; apparently praises suicide bombers and uses his own name; loudly criticizes US policies; argues (as a psychiatrist, no less) with his military patients over the worth of their sacrifices; refuses, in the name of Islam, to be photographed with female colleagues; lists his nationality as "Palestinian" in a Muslim spouse-matching program, and parades around central Texas in a fundamentalist playsuit—well, it only seems fair to call this terrorist an "*Islamist terrorist.*"

Politically Correct Denial Hurts Us

But the president won't. Despite his promise to get to all the facts. Because there's no such thing as "Islamist terrorism" in ObamaWorld.

And the Army won't. Because its senior leaders are so sick with political correctness that pandering to America-haters is safer than calling terrorism "terrorism."

And the media won't. Because they have more interest in the shooter than in our troops—despite their crocodile tears.

Maj. Nidel Malik Hasan planned this terrorist attack and executed it in cold blood. The resulting massacre was the first tragedy. The second was that he wasn't killed on the spot.

Hasan survived. Now the rest of us will have to foot his massive medical bills. Activist lawyers will get involved, claiming "harassment" drove him temporarily insane. There'll be no end of trial delays. At best, taxpayer dollars will fund his prison lifestyle for decades to come, since our politically correct Army leadership wouldn't dare pursue or carry out the death penalty.

FAST FACT

A study published in the summer 2011 issue of *Middle East Quarterly* found that of a hundred US mosques surveyed, 81 percent had imams (Muslim prayer leaders), texts, videos, or other materials that either severely or moderately advocated violence.

Maj. Hasan will be a hero to Islamist terrorists abroad and their sympathizers here. While US Muslim organizations decry his acts publicly, Hasan will be praised privately. And he'll have the last laugh.

But Hasan isn't the sole guilty party. The US Army's unforgivable political correctness is also to blame for the casualties at Ft. Hood.

Ignoring the Warning Signs

Given the myriad warning signs, it's appalling that no action was taken against a man apparently known to praise suicide bombers and openly damn US policy. But no officer in his chain of command, either at Walter Reed Army Medical Center or at Ft. Hood, had the guts to take meaningful action against a dysfunctional soldier and an incompetent doctor.

Had Hasan been a Lutheran or a Methodist, he would've been gone with the simoon [a harsh Arabian wind]. But officers fear charges of discrimination when faced with misconduct among protected minorities.

Now 12 soldiers and a security guard lie dead; 31 soldiers were wounded, 28 of them seriously. If heads don't roll in this maggot's chain of command, the Army will have shamed itself beyond moral redemption.

There's another important issue, too. How could the Army allow an obviously incompetent and dysfunctional psychiatrist to treat our troubled soldiers returning from war? An Islamist whacko is counseled for arguing with veterans who've been assigned to his care? And he's not removed from duty? What planet does the Army live on?

Islamists Comprise the Majority of Terror-Related Convictions

According to statistics released by the US Department of Justice and cataloged by the Investigative Project on Terrorism, Islamist motivation was detected in the majority of terror-related convictions between 2001 and 2010.

Taken from: "International Terrorism and Terrorism-Related Convictions 9/11/01–3/18/10." Investigation Project on Terrorism, March 9, 2011.

For the first time since I joined the Army in 1976, I'm ashamed of its dereliction of duty. The chain of command protected a budding terrorist who was waving one red flag after another. Because it was safer for careers than doing something about him.

Get ready for the apologies. We've already heard from the terrorist's family that "he's a good American." In their world, maybe he is.

But when do we, the American public, knock off the PC nonsense?

Muslims Commit Violence and Terrorism

A disgruntled Muslim soldier murdered his officers way back in 2003, in Kuwait, on the eve of Operation Iraqi Freedom. Recently? An American mullah shoots it out with the feds in Detroit. A Muslim fanatic attacks an Arkansas recruiting station. A Muslim media owner, after playing the peace card, beheads his wife. A Muslim father runs over his daughter because she's becoming too Westernized.

Wounded are evacuated after the Fort Hood shooting spree by US Army major Nidal Malik Hasan. The author argues that political correctness causes society to overlook warning signs of radical Islam's violent agenda.

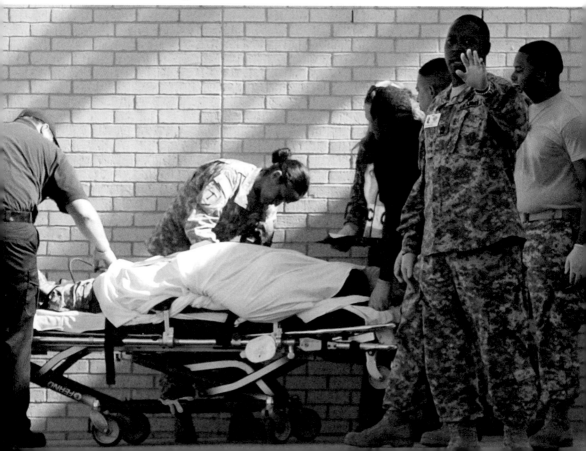

Muslim terrorist wannabes are busted again and again. And we're assured that "Islam's a religion of peace."

I guarantee you that the Obama administration's non-response to the Ft. Hood attack will mock the memory of our dead.

EVALUATING THE AUTHOR'S ARGUMENTS:

In this viewpoint Ralph Peters uses facts, examples, statements of reasoning, and persuasive writing to make his argument that Muslims are rightly linked to terrorism. He does not, however, use any quotations to support his point. If you were to rewrite this article and insert quotations, what authorities might you quote from? Where would you place them, and why?

American Policies Inspire Islamic Terrorism

Glenn Greenwald

"If we continue to bring violence to [the Muslim] world, then that part of the world . . . will continue to want to bring violence to the U.S."

In the following viewpoint Glenn Greenwald argues that American policies inspire Islamic terrorism. Greenwald explains that the United States is involved in wars in several Muslim countries, and many innocent Muslims have been killed by American weapons during the fighting. This has caused Muslims around the world to fear and hate the United States, as has its support for governments that have been accused of oppressing Muslims. Greenwald says terrorists attack the United States because of the violence and injustice it sows in Muslim countries. He concludes that anti-Americanism is a chief cause of terrorism. He urges Americans to realize that their own policies are creating the very terrorism they seek to combat.

Greenwald is known for the liberal commentary he provides to the political features of the online magazine *Salon*.

Glenn Greenwald, "Cause and Effect in the War on Terror." This article first appeared in Salon.com, at http://www.Salon.com. An online version remains in the Salon archives. Reprinted with permission.

AS YOU READ, CONSIDER THE FOLLOWING QUESTIONS:
 1. What did Faisal Shahzad tell authorities who took him into cus-
    tody at John F. Kennedy airport, according to the author?
 2. What, according to Greenwald, is the great contradiction of
    American foreign policy?
 3. What is a drone, as described by the author?

A merican discussions about what causes Terrorists to do what they do are typically conducted by ignoring the Terrorist's explanation for why he does what he does. Yesterday [June 21, 2010], Faisal Shahzad pleaded guilty in a New York federal court to attempting to detonate a car bomb in Times Square, and this Pakistani-American Muslim explained why he transformed from a financial analyst living a law-abiding, middle-class American life into a Terrorist:

> If the United States does not get out of Iraq, Afghanistan and other countries controlled by Muslims, he said, "we will be attacking U.S.," adding that Americans "only care about their people, but they don't care about the people elsewhere in the world when they die."

As soon as he was taken into custody May 3 at John F. Kennedy International Airport, onboard a flight to Dubai, the Pakistani-born Shahzad told agents that he was motivated by opposition to U.S. policy in the Muslim world, officials said.

"One of the first things he said was, 'How would you feel if people attacked the United States? You are attacking a sovereign Pakistan'," said one law enforcement official, who spoke on condition of anonymity because the interrogation reports are not public. "In the first two hours, he was talking about his desire to strike a blow against the United States for the cause."

When the federal Judge presiding over his case asked him why he would be willing to kill civilians who have nothing to do with those actions, he replied: "Well, the people select the government. We consider them all the same" (the same rationale used [by the US government] to justify the punishment of the people of Gaza for electing Hamas). When the Judge interrupted him to ask whether that includes children who might have been killed by the bomb he planted and whether he first looked around to see if there were children nearby, Shahzad replied:

> Well, the drone [unmanned bomber] hits in Afghanistan and Iraq, they don't see children, they don't see anybody. They kill women, children, they kill everybody. It's a war, and in war, they kill people. They're killing all Muslims. . . .
>
> I am part of the answer to the U.S. terrorizing the Muslim nations and the Muslim people. And, on behalf of that, I'm avenging the attack. Living in the United States, Americans only care about their own people, but they don't care about the people elsewhere in the world when they die.

Those statements are consistent with a decade's worth of emails and other private communications from Shahzad, as he railed with increasing fury against the wars in Afghanistan and Iraq, drone attacks, Israeli violence against Palestinians and Muslims generally, Guantanamo [Bay, a US detention center for suspected terrorists] and torture, and asked: "Can you tell me a way to save the oppressed? And a way to fight back when rockets are fired at us and Muslim blood flows?"

Copyright © 2011 Mike Keefe, the *Denver Post* and PoliticalCartoons.com.

This proves only what it proves. The issue here is *causation*, not justification. The great contradiction of American foreign policy is that the very actions endlessly rationalized as necessary for combating Terrorism—invading, occupying and bombing other countries, limitless interference in the Muslim world, unconditional support for Israeli aggression, vast civil liberties abridgments such as torture, renditions, due-process-free imprisonments—are the very actions that fuel the anti-American hatred which, as the U.S. Government itself has long recognized, is what causes, fuels and exacerbates the Terrorism we're ostensibly attempting to address.

It's really quite simple: if we continue to bring violence to that part of the world, then that part of the world—and those who sympathize with it—will continue to want to bring violence to the U.S. [Islamic terrorist network] Al Qaeda certainly recognizes that this is the case, as reflected in the statement it issued earlier this week [late June 2010] citing the war in Afghanistan and support for Israel as its prime grievances against the U.S. Whether that's what actually motivates that group's leaders is not the issue. They are citing those policies because they know that those grievances resonate for many Muslims, who are willing to support radical groups and support or engage in violence only because they see it as retaliation or vengeance for the violence which the U.S. is continuously perpetrating in the Muslim world (speaking of which: this week, WikiLeaks will release numerous classified documents relating to a U.S. air strike in Garani, Afghanistan that killed scores of civilians last year, while new documents reveal that substantial amounts of U.S. spending in Afghanistan end up in the hands of corrupt warlords and Taliban commanders). Clearly, there are other factors (such as religious fanaticism) that drive some people to Terrorism, but for many, it is a causal reaction to what they perceive as unjust violence being brought to them by the United States.

> **FAST FACT**
>
> University of Chicago professor Robert A. Pape found in a comprehensive study of suicide terrorism that religion is not a factor in more than 95 percent of suicide terrorist attacks. Rather, such attacks are motivated by a strategic, politically based objective: to get an occupying power to remove its troops from a homeland.

A courtroom sketch shows Faisal Shahzad speaking during his trial in 2010. Formerly a law-abiding American citizen, Shahzad says he turned to terrorism because of US policies in Iraq and Afghanistan.

Given all this, it should be anything but surprising that, as a new Pew [Research Center] poll reveals, there is a substantial drop in public support for both U.S. policies and [US president] Barack Obama personally in the Muslim world. In many Muslim countries, perceptions of the U.S.—which improved significantly upon Obama's election—have now plummeted back to [President George W.] Bush-era levels, while Obama's personal approval ratings, while still substantially higher than Bush's, are also declining, in some cases precipitously. As Pew put it:

> Roughly one year since Obama's Cairo address, America's image shows few signs of improving in the Muslim world, where opposition to key elements of U.S. foreign policy remains pervasive and many continue to perceive the U.S. as a potential military threat to their countries.

Gosh, where would they get that idea from? People generally don't like it when their countries are invaded, bombed and occupied, when they're detained without charges by a foreign power, when their internal politics are manipulated, when they see images of dead women and children as the result of remote-controlled robots from the sky. Some of them, after a breaking point is reached, get angry enough where they not only want to return the violence, but are willing to sacrifice their own lives to do so (just as was true for many Americans who enlisted after the one-day 9/11 attack). It's one thing to argue that we should continue to do these things for geopolitical gain even if it means incurring Terrorist attacks (and the endless civil liberties abridgments they engender); as amoral as that is, at least that's a cogent thought. But to pretend that Terrorism simply occurs in a vacuum, that it's mystifying why it happens, that it has nothing to do with U.S. actions in the Muslim world, requires intense self-delusion. How much more evidence is needed for that?

EVALUATING THE AUTHORS' ARGUMENTS:

Glenn Greenwald uses the story of one terrorist—Faisal Shahzad—to support his argument that American policies inspire Islamic terrorism. Yet in the following viewpoint, Andrew McCarthy uses the story of another terrorist— Omar Abdel Rahman—to support his argument that terrorism cannot be blamed on American policies. In your opinion, which of these stories better illustrates the author's point? Why? Quote from the text in your answer.

Viewpoint
6

American Policies Are Not the Reason for Islamic Terrorism

Andrew McCarthy

"Terrorism is caused, and terrorist recruitment is driven, by Islamist ideology."

In the following viewpoint Andrew McCarthy argues that American policies do not cause Islamic terrorism. In his view, Islam causes Islamic terrorism, and American policies are simply an excuse to attack. McCarthy explains that terrorists have attacked when the United States has treated its detainees harshly and when it has treated them justly; they have attacked regardless of whether terrorists have been given fair trials and despite America's attempts to deal with them humanely. From this McCarthy concludes that America's behavior has no effect on Islamic terrorists; they are only motivated, in his mind, by their twisted understanding of their religion and their desire to conquer America. McCarthy suggests that the only way in which America inspires terrorism is when it appears weak, cowardly, and vulnerable to persuasion. He warns that terrorists see a politically correct America as one that will ultimately succumb to their will and bloodthirst. The author concludes that American policies do not cause terrorism and thus the effect on terrorism should not be taken into account when policies are adopted or abandoned.

McCarthy is a columnist for the *National Review,* a conservative American magazine.

AS YOU READ, CONSIDER THE FOLLOWING QUESTIONS:
1. Who is Omar Abdel Rahman, as mentioned by McCarthy?
2. What does the term *pretext* mean as used by the author?
3. In what way does Senator Dick Durbin cause terrorism, according to McCarthy?

So we're going to shut down the detention center at the U.S. naval base on Guantanamo Bay [nicknamed Gitmo] and move the 200-plus terrorists detained there to a seldom-used civilian correctional center in Thomson, Ill. And we're doing it, the [Barack] Obama administration and [Illinois] Sen. Dick Durbin assure us, not because they want to use federal money to indemnify their home state for a white-elephant prison Illinois taxpayers should never have built, but because Guantanamo Bay simply must be closed. Gitmo, they say, causes terrorism.

Getting the Red-Carpet Treatment

It's worth remembering that the "Blind Sheikh," Omar Abdel Rahman, perhaps the world's most influential jihadist, was never held in Gitmo. Instead, he and eleven of his followers got the gold-plated due-process plan: a nine-month 1995 trial in the criminal justice system for waging war against the American people. (That's not rhetoric; that was the charge: conspiracy to levy war against the United States—Section 2384 of the federal penal code.)

The red-carpet treatment didn't begin or end with the trial. There were *Miranda* warnings [of civil rights] upon arrest (no one cooperated). Counsel was appointed, with the defendants choosing their lawyers—and, for some, Uncle Sam paid for two or more attorneys. Mountains of evidence were culled from intelligence files and duly shared with overseas terrorist organizations. The defense enjoyed a couple of years to make motions to get more discovery, to suppress evidence, and to dismiss the indictment. When things finally went to trial, there was a two-month defense case (that's much longer than most criminal trials), which allowed them to put the government on trial for its investigative tactics. There was a post-trial hearing on their motion to vacate their convictions and dismiss the case on the ground of "outrageous government misconduct." There was elaborate litigation before severe sentences were imposed: The Blind Sheikh got life imprisonment, and the other sentences ranged from 25 years to life. That was followed by a three-year appeals process, during which the court appointed new lawyers to argue that their clients had been railroaded through the incompetence of the old lawyers, while the old lawyers continued arguing that their clients had been railroaded by the malevolence of the government. Finally, when the appeals were done and the convictions upheld, the defendants began filing habeas corpus petitions—a practice that continues to this day—claiming that this or that constitutional right was infringed, or that this or that prison condition was inhumane.

So the Islamic world and its sundry terrorist bands were all very impressed with this ostentatious display of our humanity, our benign intentions, and "our values"—right? Wrong. The usual Islamist organizations claimed that America had put Islam on trial—the original slander that was refitted after 9/11 into the equally spurious charge that America is at war with Islam. In early 1997, about a year after sentencing, Sheikh Abdel Rahman's Egyptian terrorist organization, al-Gama'at al-Islamia (the Islamic Group), issued a statement declaring "all American interests legitimate targets" for "legitimate jihad" until the release of all those convicted terrorists, beginning with their beloved leader.

Swearing Vengeance

A few months later, Abdel Rahman's always-helpful American lawyers (one of whom has since been convicted of helping him run Gama'at from his U.S. prison cell) issued a statement pressuring U.S. officials to release him. "It sounds," they wrote, "like the Sheikh's condition is deteriorating and obviously could be life-threatening." On cue, Gama'at publicly warned that if any harm were to come to the sheikh, the group would "target . . . all of those Americans who participated in subjecting his life to danger." The terrorists elaborated that they considered every American official, from Pres. Bill Clinton down to "the despicable jailer," to be "partners endangering the Sheikh's life." The organization promised to do everything in its power to free Abdel Rahman.

On Nov. 17, 1997, they made good on the promise. As 58 foreign tourists visited an archeological site in Luxor, Egypt, they were set upon by six Gama'at murderers. The jihadists brutally shot and stabbed them to death—also killing several Egyptian police. The torso of one victim was slit so the terrorists could insert in it a leaflet demanding the release of the Blind Sheikh. Similar leaflets were scattered about the carnage.

Luxor was not the last of these atrocities, but it is the most savage so far, and it is the scene that should leap to mind every time some useful idiot like Senator Durbin makes the absurd claim that Guantanamo Bay must be shut down because it causes terrorism and spurs terrorist recruitment. That this claim is mindlessly repeated by high-ranking military officers and intelligence officials doesn't make it any less absurd.

The Difference Between Causes and Pretexts

We are talking about people who live in sharia states where they still stone women for adultery, apostates for daring to abandon Islam, and homosexuals for breathing. We are talking about people who riot and murder over cartoons—people who use mosques to hide weapons and Korans to transmit terrorist messages and then murder non-Muslims for purportedly defaming their religion. It makes no difference to these people that we detain Muslim terrorists in military brigs under the laws of war rather than detaining them in civilian prisons after trial in our criminal justice system.

Omar Abdel Rahman was charged with conspiracy to levy war against the United States in 1995.

After 17 years of attacks, we should have learned the difference between causes of terrorism and pretexts for terrorism. Terrorism is caused, and terrorist recruitment is driven, by Islamist ideology and by American weakness in the face of terror attacks. In that sense, Senator Durbin causes more terrorism than Gitmo ever will. Terrorist organizations are encouraged when they come to believe they can win—when they come to believe they can outlast America because we lack resolve.

The Blind Sheikh, echoed by [terrorist leader] Osama bin Laden, has promised for years that if "battalions of Islam" keep reprising Hezbollah's 1983 bombing of the Marine barracks in Beirut, and al-Qaeda's orchestration of the 1993 "Black Hawk Down" incident in Somalia, then the Americans will pack up and go home. The terrorists tell their recruits we're soft and won't defend ourselves if it gets ugly. When a U.S. senator takes to the floor of the chamber and compares heroic American troops to [Nazi leader Adolf] Hitler, [Soviet leader Joseph] Stalin, and [Cambodian leader] Pol Pot, he confirms Abdel Rahman and bin Laden's views. When he suggests that terrorism is somehow caused by locking up terrorists in a secure, offshore military facility, where they can no longer threaten Americans or anyone else, the Islamic world's fence-sitters start thinking, "The jihadists are right: America doesn't have the stomach to tough it out. If we just make it bloody enough, we can win."

Islam Causes Terrorism, Not American Policy

The only part of Gitmo that causes terrorism is its front gates, when we allow terrorists to walk out them so they can go back to the battle. Gitmo is a pretext for terrorism. Terrorists use it because, unlike us, they know it's irresponsible not to study and understand the enemy. They know the Left exercises outsize influence on the media and that the Left's key characteristic is projection.

Leftists don't like Gitmo (or the PATRIOT Act, or warrantless surveillance, or military commissions, or [former president George W.] Bush, or [former vice president Dick] Cheney, or . . .) so, presto, Gitmo becomes a "cause" of terrorism. Perversely, jihadist murderers become the vessels of our values: They're noble savages and they don't murder because they believe their religion commands them to. They do it, we're told, because of national-security policies that just happen to be the ones despised by the Left. The terrorists are onto this game even if we're not. So they snicker and say, "Oh, yes, of course, it's been Gitmo all along—that's why we do it!" They know some pointy-headed intelligence analyst, some ambitious general, some craven U.S. senator, or even some pandering American president is bound to repeat the canard until it becomes received wisdom. . . .

Terrorism Endures Despite U.S. Policy

Long before there was a Gitmo, Muslim terrorists also plotted to accomplish the release of their captured confederates, either through escape plots or extortionate terrorist attacks—like the massacre at Luxor. For them and their millions of sympathizers, the issue isn't where the jihadists are detained, or under what theory (law of war or civilian prosecution) this detention is justified. The issue is that we detain them, period. In the Muslim world, where illiteracy is rampant, there are not many scholars of American law. And, as we've already seen, even the ACLU [American Civil Liberties Union] is saying there's not a dime's worth of difference between Gitmo and the new Gitmo North at Thomson [prison in Illinois]. If that's what the lefty lawyers are saying, what do you suppose the jihadists think?

From the prison where he serves his life sentence, Abdel Rahman was able to announce to the world: "The Sheikh is calling on you, morning and evening: Oh Muslims! Oh Muslims! And he finds no respondents. It is a duty upon all the Muslims around the world to come to free the Sheikh, and to rescue him from his jail." That he was in a nice civilian jail after a nice civilian trial didn't make any difference. Of Americans, the sheikh decreed: "Muslims everywhere [must] dismember their nation, tear them apart, ruin their economy, provoke their corporations, destroy their embassies, attack their interests, sink their ships, and shoot down their planes, kill them on land, at sea, and in the air. Kill them wherever you find them." Osama bin Laden later called this the green light—the necessary Islamic fatwa—for the 9/11 attacks. It was four years before there was a Gitmo for Dick Durbin to blame. So should we shut down all the civilian prisons, too?

EVALUATING THE AUTHORS' ARGUMENTS:

Andrew McCarthy and Glenn Greenwald (author of the previous viewpoint) disagree on whether US policies are a legitimate source of terrorism. In your opinion, which author made the better argument? Why? List at least four pieces of evidence (quotes, statistics, facts, or statements of reasoning) that caused you to side with one author over the other.

Chapter 2

What Is the Status of Women in Islam?

The rights of Muslim women, including whether they are allowed to vote or drive cars, vary widely from country to country.

Islam Oppresses Women

Yasmin Alibhai-Brown

"Domestic violence destroys females in all countries, but in Muslim states, it is validated by laws and values."

In the following viewpoint Yasmin Alibhai-Brown argues that violence against Muslim women is validated by Islam, and is even legal in some Muslim countries. She recounts numerous stories from Muslim countries in which women have been beaten up, discriminated against, arrested, bought and sold, and even murdered. Alibhai-Brown explains that not only has Islam been used to justify these crimes, but the men who commit them regard themselves as very devout members of their faith who are defending it. Alibhai-Brown concludes the way Islam is currently practiced in Muslim states and immigrant communities oppresses women and violates their rights.

Alibhai-Brown is a Uganda-born Muslim journalist living in England whose columns regularly appear in London newspapers such as the *Evening Standard* and the *Independent*.

AS YOU READ, CONSIDER THE FOLLOWING QUESTIONS:

1. Who does Alibhai-Brown say divorced a fifty-year-old man, and in what country?
2. Who is Ayman Udas, as mentioned by the author?
3. What does Alibhai-Brown say has occurred in Pakistan's Swat Valley?

I am a Muslim woman and, like my late mother, free, independent, sensuous, educated, liberal, contrary and confrontational when provoked, both feminine and feminist. I style and colour my hair, wear lovely things and perfumes, appear on public platforms with men who are not related to me, shake their hands, embrace some I know well, take care of my family.

I defend Muslims persecuted by their enemies and their own kith and kin. I pray, fast, give to charity and try to be a decent human being. I also drink wine and do not lie about that, unlike so many other "good" Muslims. I am the kind of Muslim woman who maddens reactionary Muslim men and their asinine female followers. What a badge of honour.

The Subjugation of Women in Islam

Female oppression in Islamic countries is manifestly getting worse. Islam, as practiced by millions today, has lost its compassion and integrity and is entering one of the darkest of dark ages. Here is this month's [May 2009] short list of unbearable stories (imagine how many more there are which will never be known):

Iranian painter Delara Darabi, only 22 and in prison since she was 17, accused of murdering an elderly relative, was hanged last week even though she had been given a temporary stay of execution by the chief justice of the country. She phoned her mother on the day of her hanging to beg for help and the phone was snatched by a prison official who told them: "We will easily execute your daughter and there's nothing you can do about it." Her paintings reveal the cruelty to which she was subjected.

FAST FACT

A 2010 poll by the Islamic Education and Research Academy, a British organization, found that 94 percent of British non-Muslims said they thought Islam oppresses women.

Meanwhile Roxana Saberi, a 32-year-old broadcast journalist whose father is Iranian, is incarcerated in Tehran's Evin prison, accused of spying. . . . She denies this and says she has been framed because she was seen buying a bottle of wine. This intelligent, beautiful and defiant woman is on a hunger strike.

The Crisis of Women in Muslim Nations

The *Global Gender Gap Report* is published by the World Economic Forum. It ranks nations on their female citizens' educational attainment, economic participation and opportunity, health and survival, and political empowerment. Of the bottom-ranking thirty nations, twenty were Muslim, meaning that women in these nations fared poorer in these categories than women in other parts of the world.

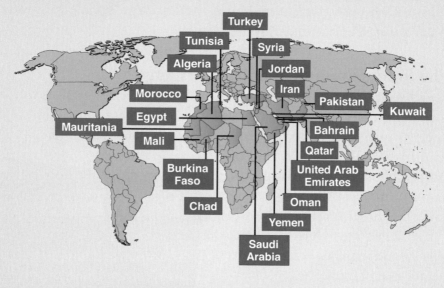

Taken from: *Global Gender Gap Report*, World Economic Forum, 2008, p.9.

Over in Saudi Arabia, an eight-year-old child has just divorced a 50-year-old man. Her father, no doubt a very devout man, sold his daughter for about £9,000 [about fourteen thousand US dollars].

Islam Validates Domestic Violence

I have been reading *Disfigured*, the story of Rania Al-Baz, a Saudi TV anchor, the first woman to have such a job, who was so badly beaten up by her abusive husband that she had to have 13 operations to re-make her once gorgeous face. Domestic violence destroys females in all countries, but in Muslim states, it is validated by laws and values.

As Al-Baz writes, "It is appalling to realise that a woman cannot walk down the street without men staring at her openly. For them she is nothing but a body without a mind, something that moves and does not think. Women are banned from studying law, from civil engineering and from the sacrosanct area of oil."

Small optimistic signs do periodically appear in this harsh desert, says Quanta A. Ahmed, a doctor who worked in Saudi Arabia and then wrote her account, *In the Land of Invisible Women*. She describes the love she finds between some husbands and wives, idealists who think better rights will come one day.

That faith in the future is echoed by Norah al-Faiz, the Deputy Minister for Women's Education, chosen in this week's *Time* magazine list of the world's most influential people. They hope because they must, I guess, even though they can see the brute forces lining up on the horizon ready to crush them by any means necessary. This country [Saudi Arabia] has spread its anti-female Wahabi Islam across the globe, its second most important export after oil.

The Right to Rape and Abuse Women

In Afghanistan Ayman Udas was a singer and songwriter who wore lipstick and appeared on TV, defying her family. She was a divorced mother of two who had remarried. Ten days after this she was shot dead, allegedly by her brothers, who must think they are upright moral upholders with places reserved in paradise. In March President [Hamid] Karzai gave monstrous tribal leaders what they demanded, absolute control over wives by husbands and the right to rape them on the marital bed. Protests by brave women in that country and international outrage has forced him to step back from this commitment but there is concern that he is too weak to hold out, and once again women will become the personal and political playthings of men.

Let's [go] to Pakistan then, shall we, the country that once elected a woman head of state. The divinely beautiful Swat Valley has, for reasons of political expediency, been handed over to the Taliban, and there they have blown up over a hundred schools for girls and regularly flog young females on the streets. The girls are shrouded and forbidden to scream because the female voice has the potential to arouse desire. Or pity perhaps.

In her book Between Two Worlds, *Iranian American journalist Roxana Saberi (pictured) tells how she was imprisoned in Iran for allegedly being a US spy.*

Muslim Women Are Forced to Be Ghosts

I am aware that my words will help confirm the pernicious prejudices that fester in the minds of those who despise Islam. Yet to conceal or excuse the violations would be to condone and encourage them. There have been enlightened times when some Muslim civilisations honoured and cherished females. This is not one of them. Across the West—for a host of reasons—millions of Muslims are embracing backward practices. In the UK young girls—some so young that they are still in push chairs—are covered up in hijabs [head scarves]. Disgracefully, there are always vocal Muslim women who seek to justify honour killings, forced marriages, inequality, polygamy and childhood betrothals. Why are large numbers of Muslim men so terrorised by the female body and spirit? Why do Muslim women encourage this savage paranoia?

I look out of my study at the common and see a wife fully burkaed [wearing a covering over the face and body] on a sunny day. She sits still. Her children and husband run around, laughing, playing cricket. She sits still, dead, buried, a ghost. She is complicit in her own degradation, as are countless others. Their acquiescence in a free democracy is a crime against their sisters who have no such choices in Saudi Arabia, Iran, Afghanistan and elsewhere.

Al-Baz says: "I am a disruptive presence because I give women ideas." Me too. To transgress against diehard obscurantists and their unholy rules is an inescapable sacred duty. Yet how pathetic that sounds. Progressive believers tilt at windmills driven by ferocious winds of self-righteousness. Our arms and legs weaken and we are brought to our knees. I fear there is only worse to come.

EVALUATING THE AUTHORS' ARGUMENTS:

In this viewpoint Yasmin Alibhai-Brown describes many terrible offenses committed against women by Muslim men in Muslim nations. Yet in the following viewpoint, the Islamic Center for PEACE argues that Islam grants women economic, social, family, and other kinds of rights. How does this view of Islam jibe with the poor treatment of Muslim women described by Alibhai-Brown? After reading both texts, explain your opinion of whether Islam oppresses women, grants them rights, or offers them something in between.

Islam Grants Women Rights

Islamic Center for PEACE

"Islam elevated the position of women in society and treated them on an equal footing with men."

The Islamic Center for PEACE is a Florida-based organization that promotes Islam among the general public. It frequently collaborates with churches and synagogues to foster healthy and productive interfaith dialogues. In the following viewpoint it argues that women enjoy high status and multiple rights under Islam. The organization explains that in Islam, women are viewed as equal to men. Islam offers them equal education, free speech, civic participation, and a wide range of economic rights. If contemporary Muslim women do not enjoy all of these rights, the center says, that is the fault of the governments of the nations in which they live, and does not reflect upon Islam itself. The Islamic Center for PEACE concludes that Islam has been a source of liberation, equality, and justice for women since its origins.

AS YOU READ, CONSIDER THE FOLLOWING QUESTIONS:

1. What is the text of Qur'an 49:13 and which of the author's points is it intended to support?
2. What marriage rights does the author say Islam grants to women?
3. What inheritance rights does the author say Islam grants to women?

"Status of Women in Islam" reprinted with permission from www.whyislam.org. For additional information, please visit www.whyislam.org or call our toll-free hotline 1-877-Whyislam.

The status of women in Islam is an issue that is pertinent in present times; both due to the divergence of cultural practices in the Muslim world from the Islamic perspective and the erroneous perception in the West, that Islam subjugates womenfolk.

A dispassionate study of the primary sources of Islam, along with an analysis of the position of women in societies where Islam was implemented, actually proves that for women Islam is a special blessing.

Islam Is a Blessing for Women

"Prior to Islam," write the authors of *The Cultural Atlas of Islam*, "a woman was regarded by her parents as a threat to family honor and hence worthy of burial alive at infancy. As an adult, she was a sex object that could be bought, sold and inherited. From this position of inferiority and legal incapacity, Islam raised women to a position of influence and prestige in family and society."

The rights and responsibilities of women are equal to those of men but they are not necessarily identical. This difference is understandable because men and women are different, in their physiological and psychological make-up. With this distinction in mind, there is no room for a Muslim to imagine that women are inferior to men. Thus it is perhaps more apt to refer to the Islamic approach on gender relations, as one of "equity" rather than the commonly used word "equality", which could be misunderstood to mean equality in every minute aspect of life, rather than overall equality.

The Qur'an Discusses the Equality of Women

The sacred text of the Glorious Qur'an and the history of early Muslims bear witness to the fact that women are considered as vital to life as men.

Islam refuted the idea that Eve tempted Adam to disobey God, and thus caused his downfall. The Qur'an says that they both disobeyed, and negates the idea that women are a source of evil.

In a world where women were no more than objects of sexual gratification for men, and at a time when the religious circles argued over whether women were human or not, possessing souls, Islam proclaimed:

"O Mankind! We created you from a single (pair) of a male and a female." [Al-Qur'an 49:13]

An Iraqi woman displays her ink-stained finger after casting her vote in Iraq's 2010 elections.

"O Mankind! Reverence your Guardian-Lord, Who created you from a single person, created of like nature his mate, from them scattered countless men and women. Fear Allah, through whom you demand your mutual rights and reverence the wombs (that bore you), for Allah ever watches over you." [Al-Qur'an 4:1]

Men and women are of the same family, and as such have similar rights and duties, and their Lord promises them in the Glorious Qur'an:

"Never will I waste the work of a worker among you, whether male or female, the one of you being from the other." [Al-Qur'an 3:195]

Thus, in the Islamic tradition, a woman has an independent identity. She is a responsible being in her own right and carries the burden of her moral and spiritual obligations.

Islam Grants Women Multiple Rights

Women have as much right to education as men do. Almost fourteen centuries ago, Prophet Muhammad declared that the pursuit of knowledge is incumbent on every Muslim, male and female. This declaration was very clear and was largely implemented by Muslims throughout history.

Islam elevated the position of women in society and treated them on an equal footing with men, and in some cases, as a mother for instance, clearly gave them precedence over men. Thus when a man asked Prophet Muhammad: "Who is most entitled to be treated with the best companionship by me?" the prophet replied, "Your mother." The man asked, "Who is next? The Prophet said, "Your mother." Again the man asked, "Who is next?" The Prophet repeated, "Your mother." The man asked for a fourth time, "Who is next?" The Prophet then replied, "Your father."

On another occasion, when a man came to the Prophet, and expressed the desire to join a military expedition, the Prophet asked him if he had a mother. When he replied that he had, the Prophet advised him, "Stay with her, for Paradise is at her feet."

As daughters, women have a right to just and equitable treatment from their parents. The Prophet gave glad tidings to those who did not insult their daughters or favored sons over daughters.

A woman has the right to accept or reject marriage proposals, and her consent is a prerequisite to the validity of the marriage contract. A marriage is based on mutual peace, love and compassion. Dr. Jamal Badawl, a Canadian Islamic scholar, states in his book *Gender Equity in Islam:*

"The husband is responsible for the maintenance, protection and overall leadership of the family within the framework of consultation and kindness. The mutuality and complementarity of husband and wife does not mean 'subservience' by either party to the other. Prophet Muhammad helped with household chores, although the responsibilities he bore and the issues he faced in the community were immense."

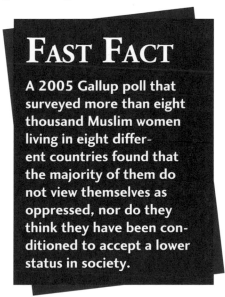

FAST FACT

A 2005 Gallup poll that surveyed more than eight thousand Muslim women living in eight different countries found that the majority of them do not view themselves as oppressed, nor do they think they have been conditioned to accept a lower status in society.

The responsibility of maintaining social and moral values lies on both men and women. Both must refrain from all deeds and gestures that might stir the passions of people other than their legitimate spouses or cause evil suspicion of their morality.

Freedom of Expression

Women are entitled to freedom of expression just as men are. Among the early Muslims, women participated in public life, especially in times of emergencies. It is reported in the Qur'an and in history that women not only expressed their opinion freely but also argued and participated in serious discussions with the Prophet himself as well as with other Muslim leaders. They were not shut behind iron bars or considered worthless.

Islam grants women equal rights to contract, to enterprise, to earn and possess independently. A woman's life, her property and her honor are as sacred as those of a man. If she commits any offense, her penalty is no less or more than of a man's in a similar case. If she is wronged or harmed, she gets due compensation equal to what a man in her position would get.

Islam has given women a share of inheritance. Before Islam, women were not only deprived of that share, but were themselves considered as property to be inherited by men. Out of that transferable property Islam made an heir, acknowledging the inherent individuality of women. Whether the woman is a wife or mother, a sister or daughter, she receives a certain share of the deceased kin's property, a share that depends on her degree of relationship to the deceased and the number of heirs. This share is hers, and no one can take it away or disinherit her. Even if the deceased wishes to deprive her by making a will to other relations or in favor of any other cause, the Law will not allow him to do so.

Women are exempt from all financial liabilities. As a wife, a woman is entitled to demand of her prospective husband a suitable dowry that will be her own. She is entitled to complete provision and total maintenance by the husband. She does not have to work or share with her husband the family expenses. She is free to retain, after marriage, whatever she possessed before it, and the husband has no right whatsoever to any of her belongings. As a daughter or sister she is entitled to security and provision by the father and brother respectively. That

Women's Rights in Islam

The Koran offers women a variety of economic, social, and political rights, including:

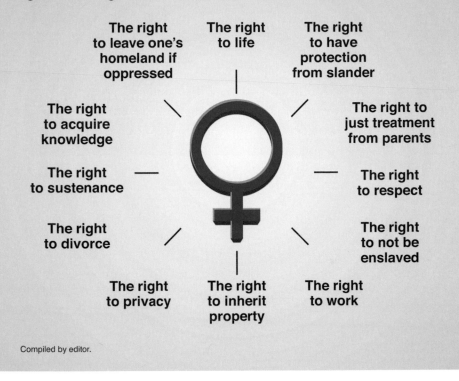

The right to leave one's homeland if oppressed

The right to life

The right to have protection from slander

The right to acquire knowledge

The right to just treatment from parents

The right to sustenance

The right to respect

The right to divorce

The right to not be enslaved

The right to privacy

The right to inherit property

The right to work

Compiled by editor.

is her privilege. If she wishes to work or be self-supporting and participate in handling the family responsibilities, she is quite free to do so, provided her integrity and honor are safeguarded.

The Status of Women in Islam Is High

It is thus clear that the status of women in Islam is very high. Islam has granted them rights that match beautifully with their duties. What Islam has established for women is that which suits their nature, gives them full security and protects them against disgraceful circumstances and uncertain channels of life.

There does exist a gap between the rights of women outlined in the Qur'an, and the prevalent reality in the Muslim world. However, images of Muslim women as ignorant, oppressed and submissive are stereotypical and do no justice to the large number of Muslim women whose firm conviction in the Islamic concepts of family cohesiveness and happiness, and their own individuality, ensures their sense of self-fulfillment.

EVALUATING THE AUTHOR'S ARGUMENTS:

One of the rights discussed by the Islamic Center for PEACE is the right of women to be "exempt from all financial duties." Explain what the author means by this. In your opinion, is this a desirable right? Why or why not?

The Veil Oppresses Women

Mona Eltahaway

"The burqa is an affront to Muslim women."

In the following viewpoint Mona Eltahaway argues that full-body veils called burkas, or burqas, oppress women and should not be a part of Islam. She explains the practice of veiling women stems from old tribal cultures, not from the religion of Islam. She says the veil has been used by Islamic extremists to erase women, obscure their identity, and prevent them from participating equally in society. For all of these reasons she thinks burkas and other kinds of repressive veils should be banned by governments and rejected by Muslims.

Eltahaway is an Egyptian-born commentator on Arab and Muslim issues.

AS YOU READ, CONSIDER THE FOLLOWING QUESTIONS:

1. Who is Nicolas Sarkozy and why does the author mention him?
2. What is different, in Eltahaway's opinion, about wearing a burqa in Copenhagen, Denmark, and wearing one in Saudi Arabia?
3. What is wrong with comparing women to a diamond ring, according to the author?

I am a Muslim, I am a feminist and I detest the full-body veil, known as a niqab or burqa. It erases women from society and has nothing to do with Islam but everything to do with the hatred for women at the heart of the extremist ideology that preaches it.

We must not sacrifice women at the altar of political correctness or in the name of fighting a growingly powerful right wing that Muslims face in countries where they live as a minority.

Many Politicians Agree

As disagreeable as I often find French President Nicolas Sarkozy, he was right when he said recently, "The burqa is not a religious sign, it is a sign of the subjugation, of the submission of women. I want to say solemnly that it will not be welcome on our territory." It should not be welcome anywhere, I would add.

Yet his words have inspired attempts to defend the indefensible— the erasure of women.

> **FAST FACT**
>
> As of 2011 France and Belgium had banned women from wearing burkas, niqabs, or any other clothing that covers their faces, and a ban was under way in Italy. Denmark, Germany, and the Netherlands have considered similar laws.

Some have argued that Sarkozy's right-leaning, anti-Muslim bias was behind his opposition to the burqa. But I would remind them of comments in 2006 by the then-British House of Commons leader Jack Straw, who said the burqa prevents communication. He was right, and he was hardly a right-winger—and yet he too was attacked for daring to speak out against the burqa.

The racism and discrimination that Muslim minorities face in many countries—such as France, which has the largest Muslim community in Europe, and Britain, where two members of the xenophobic British National Party were shamefully elected to the European Parliament—are very real.

But the best way to support Muslim women would be to say we oppose both racist Islamophobes and the burqa. We've been silent on too many things out of fear we'll arm the right wing.

Women in Afghanistan are shown wearing burkas. Women's rights groups say the burka is an oppressive relic from old tribal customs and not a religious requirement.

An Affront to Muslim Women

The best way to debunk the burqa as an expression of Muslim faith is to listen to Muslims who oppose it. At the time of Mr. Straw's comments, a controversy erupted when a university dean in Egypt warned students they would not be able to stay at college dorms unless they removed their burqa. The dean cited security grounds, saying that men disguised as women in burqa could slip into the female dorms.

Soad Saleh, a professor of Islamic law and former dean of the women's faculty of Islamic studies at Al-Azhar University—hardly a liberal, said the burqa had nothing to do with Islam. It was but an old Bedouin tradition.

It is sad to see a strange ambivalence toward the burqa from many of my fellow Muslims and others who claim to support us. They will take on everything—the right wing, Islamophobia, Mr. Straw, Mr. Sarkozy—rather than come out and plainly state that the burqa is an affront to Muslim women.

"I Am Not Candy"

I blame such reluctance on the success of the ultra-conservative Salafi ideology—practiced most famously in Saudi Arabia—in leaving its

Support for a Ban on Veils That Cover the Whole Face

Several European nations support banning full-body veils. France made them illegal in 2010 because they were determined to violate women's rights and to interfere with social integration and communication.

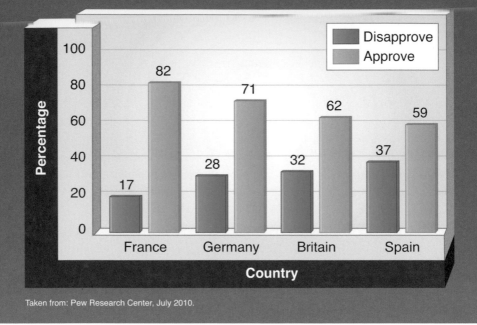

Taken from: Pew Research Center, July 2010.

imprimatur on Islam globally by persuading too many Muslims that it is the purest and highest form of our faith.

It's one thing to argue about the burqa in a country like Saudi Arabia—where I lived for six years and where women are treated like children—but it is utterly dispiriting to have those same arguments in a country where women's rights have long been enshrined. When I first saw a woman in a burqa in Copenhagen [Denmark] I was horrified.

I wore a headscarf for nine years. An argument I had on the Cairo subway with a woman who wore a burqa helped seal for good my refusal to defend it. Dressed in black from head to toe, the woman asked me why I did not wear the burqa. I pointed to my headscarf and asked her "Is this not enough?"

"If you wanted a piece of candy, would you choose an unwrapped piece or one that came in a wrapper?" she asked.

"I am not candy," I answered. "Women are not candy."

"A Woman Who Wears It Is Erased"

I have since heard arguments made for the burqa in which the woman is portrayed as a diamond ring or a precious stone that needs to be hidden to prove her "worth." Unless we challenge it, the burqa—and by extension the erasure of women—becomes the pinnacle of piety.

It is not about comparing burqas to bikinis, as some claim. I used to compare my headscarf to a miniskirt, the two being essentially two sides to the same coin of a woman's body. The burqa is something else altogether: A woman who wears it is erased.

A bizarre political correctness has tied the tongues of those who would normally rally to women's rights. One blogger, a woman, lamented that "Sarkozy's anti-burqa stance deprives women of identity." It's precisely the opposite: It's the burqa that deprives a woman of identity.

Why do women in Muslim-minority communities wear the burqa? Sarkozy touched on one reason when he admitted his country's integration model wasn't working any more because it doesn't give immigrants and their French-born-children a fair chance.

Depriving Women of Their Identity

But the Muslim community must ask itself the same question: Why the silence as some of our women fade into black either as a form of identity politics, a protest against the state or out of acquiescence to Salafism?

As a Muslim woman and a feminist I would ban the burqa.

EVALUATING THE AUTHOR'S ARGUMENTS:

In making her argument, Mona Eltahaway says "I am not candy. Women are not candy." In a paragraph or two, explain what she means by this and how it relates to conversations about the veil. Then, state your own opinion about veiling: Do you think it oppresses women? Why or why not?

The Veil Does Not Necessarily Oppress Women

Naomi Wolf

"Westerners should recognise that when a woman . . . chooses a veil, it is not necessarily a sign of her repression."

In the following viewpoint Naomi Wolf argues that veiling offers Muslim women an enviable sense of security, self-worth, and freedom. She explains that veiled women are free from the scrutiny and degradation that often accompany skimpy and revealing Western outfits. They do not feel bad about their bodies and, because veils remove an element of sexual tension from interactions, women are valued for their thoughts and ideas rather than their cleavage or hair length. Wolf says veiling does not suppress sexuality. It merely channels it to more appropriate places, such as private moments with a spouse. She concludes that veiling does not oppress women but rather frees them from cultures increasingly obsessed with sex.

Wolf is cofounder of the American Freedom Campaign, an American democracy movement. She is also the author of the book *Give Me Liberty: How to Become an American Revolutionary.*

AS YOU READ, CONSIDER THE FOLLOWING QUESTIONS:
  1. According to Wolf, how do Muslim women feel when confronted with ads that feature scantily clad models?
  2. How did the author feel when she donned a loose-fitting outfit and veil in a Moroccan bazaar?
  3. What do Muslim and Orthodox Jewish women report enjoying higher levels of, according to Wolf?

A woman swathed in black to her ankles, wearing a headscarf or a full chador, walks down a European or North American street, surrounded by other women in halter tops, miniskirts and short shorts. She passes under immense billboards on which other women swoon in sexual ecstasy, cavort in lingerie or simply stretch out languorously, almost fully naked. Could this image be any more iconic of the discomfort the West has with the social mores of Islam, and vice versa?

Ideological battles are often waged with women's bodies as their emblems, and Western Islamophobia is no exception. When France banned headscarves in schools, it used the hijab [head scarf] as a proxy for Western values in general, including the appropriate status of women. When Americans were being prepared for the invasion of Afghanistan, the Taliban were demonised for denying cosmetics and hair colour to women; when the Taliban were overthrown, Western writers often noted that women had taken off their scarves.

But are we in the West radically misinterpreting Muslim sexual mores, particularly the meaning to many Muslim women of being veiled or wearing the chador? And are we blind to our own markers of the oppression and control of women?

In Touch with Their Sensuality

The West interprets veiling as repression of women and suppression of their sexuality. But when I travelled in Muslim countries and was invited to join a discussion in women-only settings within Muslim homes, I learned that Muslim attitudes toward women's appearance and sexuality are not rooted in repression, but in a strong sense of public versus private, of what is due to God and what is due to one's

The author maintains that Muslim attitudes toward women's sexuality, including the practice of veiling, are rooted not in repression, but in a strong sense of privacy and appropriateness.

husband. It is not that Islam suppresses sexuality, but that it embodies a strongly developed sense of its appropriate channelling—toward marriage, the bonds that sustain family life, and the attachment that secures a home.

Outside the walls of the typical Muslim households that I visited in Morocco, Jordan, and Egypt, all was demureness and propriety. But inside, women were as interested in allure, seduction and pleasure as women anywhere in the world.

At home, in the context of marital intimacy, Victoria's Secret, elegant fashion and skin care lotions abounded. The bridal videos that I was shown, with the sensuous dancing that the bride learns as part of what makes her a wonderful wife, and which she proudly displays for her bridegroom, suggested that sensuality was not alien to Muslim women. Rather, pleasure and sexuality, both male and female, should not be displayed promiscuously—and possibly destructively—for all to see.

A Source of Freedom

Indeed, many Muslim women I spoke with did not feel at all subjugated by the chador or the headscarf. On the contrary, they felt liberated from what they experienced as the intrusive, commodifying, basely sexualising Western gaze. Many women said something like this: "When I wear Western clothes, men stare at me, objectify me, or I am always measuring myself against the standards of models in magazines, which are hard to live up to—and even harder as you get older, not to mention how tiring it can be to be on display all the time. When I wear my headscarf or chador, people relate to me as an individual, not an object; I feel respected." This may not be expressed in a traditional Western feminist set of images, but it is a recognisably Western feminist set of feelings.

I experienced it myself. I put on a shalwar kameez [a loose tunic and pants] and a headscarf in Morocco for a trip to the bazaar. Yes, some of the warmth I encountered was probably from the novelty of seeing a Westerner so clothed; but, as I moved about the market—the curve of my breasts covered, the shape of my legs obscured, my long hair not flying about me—I felt a novel sense of calm and serenity. I felt, yes, in certain ways, free.

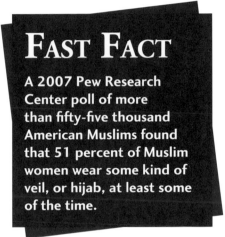

Keeping Sexuality Private

Nor are Muslim women alone. The Western Christian tradition portrays all sexuality, even married sexuality, as sinful. Islam and Judaism never had that same kind of mind-body split. So, in both cultures, sexuality channeled into marriage and family life is seen as a source of great blessing, sanctioned by God.

This may explain why both Muslim and Orthodox Jewish women [who cover their hair] not only describe a sense of being liberated by their modest clothing and covered hair, but also express much higher levels of sensual joy in their married lives than is common in the West.

When sexuality is kept private and directed in ways seen as sacred—and when one's husband isn't seeing his wife (or other women) half-naked all day long—one can feel great power and intensity when the headscarf or the chador comes off in the home.

Among healthy young men in the West, who grow up on pornography and sexual imagery on every street corner, reduced libido is a growing epidemic, so it is easy to imagine the power that sexuality can carry in a more modest culture. And it is worth understanding the positive experiences that women—and men—can have in cultures where sexuality is more conservatively directed.

Reconsidering "Female Freedom"

I do not mean to dismiss the many women leaders in the Muslim world who regard veiling as a means of controlling women. Choice is everything. But Westerners should recognise that when a woman in France or Britain chooses a veil, it is not necessarily a sign of her repression. And, more importantly, when you choose your own miniskirt and halter top—in a Western culture in which women are not so free to age, to be respected as mothers, workers or spiritual beings, and to disregard Madison Avenue—it's worth thinking in a more nuanced way about what female freedom really means.

EVALUATING THE AUTHORS' ARGUMENTS:

Naomi Wolf and Mona Eltahaway (author of the previous viewpoint) come to very different conclusions about what the full-body veil offers women. Wolf claims it liberates women and helps them be appreciated for their minds rather than their bodies. Eltahaway says it oppresses women by erasing their identities and silencing them. After reading both viewpoints, with which author do you agree, and why? Quote from the text that persuaded you in your answer.

Islam Condones Honor Killings

Valentina Colombo

"Honor killing . . . can find justification in the Koran and in Islamic tradition."

Valentina Colombo is a senior fellow at the European Foundation for Democracy. She also teaches Geopolitics of the Islamic World at the European University in Rome. In the following viewpoint she argues that honor killings are inherently Islamic. She contends that they are part of Muslim culture and society and justified by the faith itself. To prove this, she cites data that show the majority of honor killings are committed by Muslim men who say they killed to defend their faith. Other killers invoked Islamic statements or ideas as they celebrated their actions. Colombo says Muslims are in denial about the Islamic link to honor killing. She applauds Muslims who have acted to condemn honor killings without denying their relationship to Islam.

AS YOU READ, CONSIDER THE FOLLOWING QUESTIONS:
1. Who is Du'a al-Aswad and how does she factor into the author's argument?
2. What percent of honor killings committed in the West does Colombo say were committed by Muslim men?
3. What is the text of Koran Sura IV and how does it factor into the author's argument?

Valentina Colombo, "Islam and Honor Killings," *Hudson NY,* September 28, 2009. All rights reserved. Reproduced by permission.

L ast September 15th [2009] Sanaa Dafani, an 18 year old girl of Moroccan origin, was killed by her father because she loved a 31 year old Italian. The father was immediately arrested while the mother tried to find a reason for his act: "My husband loved Sanaa. Maybe she was wrong. I could forgive my husband. Yes, I could. He is my husband, my sons' father. Sanaa dressed and ate in a proper way, but he did not want her to go out in the evening with bad boys or friends. My husband loved Sanaa. Maybe she was wrong. He always sent her messages: come back home. He wanted her beside him."

Almost the same words were pronounced by Hina Saleem's mother three years ago. On August 11th, 2006, Hina, a 21 year old girl of Pakistani origin, was slain by her father because she wanted to live like a Westerner and had decided to go and live with a non-Muslim man. On April 7th, 2007, Du'a al-Aswad, a 17 year old Kurdish girl of Yazidi faith, was stoned by a raging crowd in Iraq because apparently she had offended her family's honor. In Turkey, almost 200 honor killings are committed every year, in Syria, between 200 and 300. In Pakistan there are between 800 and 1000 honor killings every year. These numbers are sad and worrisome.

The problem of honor killings is known; what is less known is that research made by the American psychologist Phyllis Chesler shows that in the period 1989–2009, there have been 87 victims in the West and 130 in the Third World—and that 84% of honor killings committed in the West are by Muslims. When Chesler exposed these results last September during the International Conference on Violence against Women, she was immediately reminded by the Egyptian minister, Moushira al-Khattab, that Islam does not allow this; that the problem are some Muslims and that the Prophet Muhammad respected women.

Muslims Try to Deny the Link

Even radical Muslims point out that honor killing does not belong to Islam. In a document issued by the Muslim Council of Britain—after some honor killings in the UK [United Kingdom]—you can read the following: "Let us consider the example of the Muslim man recently given a life sentence for slitting his daughter's throat in an 'Honour Killing' after she began dating a Christian. This is a tragic story of irreconcilable cultural differences between a father who had a traditional 'Muslim' upbringing, values and background and a daughter who had adopted non-Islamic cultural life. But a devout Muslim who understands their religion correctly would certainly never take another life. In reality, such tragedies have nothing to do with true faith." These words are the typical beating-about-the-bush of Islamic extremists—which have to be read between the lines. The document acknowledges the Muslim background of these homicides and underlines the culpability of the girls because they left behind their Islamic principles. Muslim women cannot marry Christian men unless he converts to Islam. All this does not imply a homicide, but it clearly shows that in Islam there is no freedom of choice, at least for women.

Even the words of sheikh Atiyyah Saqr, former head of Al-Azhar Fatwa Committee in Cairo, are very ambiguous: "Like all other religions, Islam strictly prohibits murder and killing without legal justification. Allah, Most High, says, "Who so slayeth a believer of set purpose, his reward is Hell forever. Allah is wroth against him and He hath cursed him and prepared for him an awful doom." (An-Nisa': 93) The so-called "honor killing" is based on ignorance and disregard of morals and laws, which cannot be abolished except by disciplinary punishments. It goes without saying that people are not entitled to take the law in their own hands, for it's the responsibility of the Muslim State and its concerned bodies to maintain peace, security, etc., and to prevent chaos and disorder from creeping into the Muslim society." In other words the Islamic state, following the sharia [Muslim law], even though it does not accept honor killings, allows the stoning of the adulteress. Honor killing is replaced with "legal" death.

The Islamic Basis for Honor Killings

Honor killing is the product of a male chauvinist society; it can find justification in the Koran and in Islamic tradition. Du'a's death

North American Victims of Honor Killings

Honor killing victims have usually been murdered because their families think they have gone against Islam's idea of modesty, have become "too Western," or seek a forbidden level of independence.

Victim Name (age)	Year, Location	Perpetrators' Names, Origin	Motive	Method
Palestina Isa (16)	1989 St. Louis, MO	Maria & Zein Isa, parents, sisters also encouraged it / West Bank. (M)	"Too American."	Stabbed thirteen times by father as her mother held her down.
Methal Dayem (22)	1999 Cleveland, OH	Yezen Dayem, Musa Saleh, cousins / West Bank. (M)	Refused to marry her cousin; attended college; sought independent career; drove her own car.	Two cousins allegedly shot and choked her.
Lubaina Bhatti Ahmed (39)	1999 St. Clairsville, OH	Nawaz Ahmed, estranged husband / West Bank. (M)	Filed for divorce.	Throat cut; her father, sister and sister's young child's throat also cut.
Farah Khan (5)	1999 Toronto, ON, Canada	Muhammed Khan, father, and Kaneez Fatma, stepmother / unknown region. (M)	Suspected child was not his biologically.	Father and step-mother cut her throat, dismembered her body.
Jawinder "Jassi" Kaur (25)	2000 Pakistan	Gang of men hired by Malkiat Kaur, mother, and Surjit Sing Badesha, uncle / Canada / Pakistan. (S)	Against her parents' wishes, married a man who was of inferior financial status.	Kidnapped, throat slashed.
Shahpara Sayeed (33)	2000 Chicago, IL	Mohammad Harroon, husband / Pakistan. (M)	Motive unclear.	Burned alive.
Maryln Hassan (29)	2002 Jersey City, NJ	Alim Hassan, husband / Guyana (Hindu wife). (M)	His wife refused to convert from Hinduism to Islam.	Husband, an auto mechanic, stabbed wife (and the twins in her womb), the wife's sister, and the wife's mother.
Amandeep Sing Atwal (17)	2003 British Columbia, BC, Canada	Rajinder Singh Atwal, father / East Indies. (S)	Wanted daughter to end relationship with non-Sikh classmate, Todd McIsaac.	Father stabbed daughter eleven times.
Hatice Peltek (39)	2004 Scottsville, NY	Ismail Peltek, husband / Turkey (M)	Had been molested by brother-in-law.	Stabbed, bludgeoned with hammer along with daughters.
Aqsa Parvez (16)	2007 Toronto, ON, Canada	Muhammad Parvez, father, Waqas Parvez, brother (M) / unknown region	Refusing to wear hijab.	Strangled.
Amina Said (17)	2008 Irving, TX	Yaser Said, father; mother assisted / Egypt (M)	Upset by her "Western" ways.	Shot.
Sarah Said (18)	2008 Irving, TX	Yaser Said, father; mother assisted / Egypt (M)	Upset by her "Western" ways.	Shot.
Fauzia Mohammed (19)	2008 Henrietta, NY	Goaded by mother, Waheed Allah Mohammed, brother / Afghanistan (M)	Too "Western," immodest clothing, planned to attend college.	Stabbed.
Sandeela Kanwal (25)	2008 Atlanta, GA	Chaudry Rashid, father / Pakistan (M)	Filed for divorce after arranged marriage.	Strangled.

Taken from: Phyllis Chesler, "Are Honor Killings Simply Domestic Violence?," *Middle East Quarterly*, Spring 2009, pp.61–69.

confirms what has just been said. The Kurdish girl was not only stoned, but her body was mutilated and covered with stones. At the end the crowd started shouting "Allahu akbar", "God is greatest", and reciting the shahada, that is the Islamic profession of faith.

One year after Du'a's murder, the Saudi activist, Wajeha al-Huwaider, wrote: "Had Du'a been an animal, someone would have [probably] taken notice and tried to rescue her from these inhuman men. But she was a woman, and in the Greater East, the life of a woman is worth far less than the life of an animal. [. . .] All those who believe that honor [resides] in the woman's body are potential murderers, and [could] someday murder a woman when their false sense of honor is aroused. All those who agree that a man has the right

Human rights activists in Lahore, Pakistan, demonstrate against the practice of honor killings. In 2008 five women were shot and buried alive after insisting on marrying men of their choice.

to murder a woman, or to cause her physical harm [for the sake of preserving] his honor, are potential killers."

To all this one can add that in most Islamic countries laws which counteract honor killings almost do not exist. For instance, on July 1st, 2009, Syrian President Bashar al-Assad abolished Article 548 of the Penal Code, which had waived punishment for a man found to have killed a female family member in a case "provoked" by "illegitimate sex acts," as well as for a husband who killed his wife because of an extramarital affair. The article also lowered penalties if a killing were found to be based on a "suspicious state" concerning a female family member. The article that replaced it still allows for mitigated punishment for "honor killings," but requires a sentence of at least two years. The new text of Article 548 reads: "He who catches his wife, sister, mother or daughter by surprise, engaging in an illegitimate sexual act and kills or injures them unintentionally must serve a minimum of two years in prison." In the previous text, the killer benefited from a complete "exemption of penalty". We could say that something is starting to change, but we are still very far away from a true fight of honor killings in the country.

Islam's Role Cannot Be Denied

Islam and the male chauvinist tradition are the worst enemies of Muslim women. It cannot be denied, as the Egyptian Minister tried to do, that Islam has something to do with this. In the Koran, in Sura IV, we read: "Should any of your women commit some sexual offence, collect evidence about them from four [persons] among yourselves. If they so testify, then confine the women to their houses until death claims them or God grants them some other way out" and "Admonish those women whose surliness you fear, and leave them alone in their beds, and [even] beat them [if necessary]". If the Koran does not quote honor killings, it can be of some use to justify them. The Swiss-Yemeni liberal intellectual, Elham Manea, is perfectly right when she says that Muslims should admit that there is a problem concerning women in general and honor killings in particular in Islam itself. This is not meant to be anti-Islamic. Manea is a secular Muslim who does not wish to conceal problems; on the contrary, she wishes to face and solve them to improve the condition of Muslim women.

Only in this way can the West and the Muslim world fight violence against women who only want to be free, as the Lebanese poet Joumana Haddad describes in a poem of hers: "They put me in a cage so that/My freedom may be a gift from them,/And I have to thank them and obey./But I am free before them, after them,/With them, without them. [. . .] I am a woman./They think they own my freedom./I let them think so,/And I happen".

EVALUATING THE AUTHOR'S ARGUMENTS:

Valentina Colombo quotes from several sources to support the points she makes in her essay. Make a list of everyone she quotes, including their credentials and the nature of their comments. Then, analyze her sources—are they credible? Are they well qualified to speak on this subject? What specific points do they support?

Viewpoint

6

Islam Does Not Condone Honor Killings

Kamran Pasha

"[Honor killing] is one of the ugly elements of pre-Islamic Arabian culture that continues to reassert itself, despite the Prophet's efforts to eradicate the practice."

In the following viewpoint Kamran Pasha argues that honor killing is not Islamic. He explains that historically, Islam has protected women, granted them rights, and prohibited their abuse. Even the Prophet Muhammad, he says, tried to outlaw honor killings. Such violence endures because honor killings are an ancient cultural practice that continue to be part of certain cultures that have also adopted Islam, Pasha says. He says Islam is a beautiful, peaceful religion that could never condone something as horrible as honor killings.

Pasha is a screenwriter and the author of *Mother of the Believers,* a book about the birth of Islam as told by the Prophet Muhammad's teenage wife Aisha.

AS YOU READ, CONSIDER THE FOLLOWING QUESTIONS:

1. What does the author say began as a proto-feminist movement?
2. What was one of the first practices outlawed by the Prophet Muhammad, according to Pasha?
3. What, in Pasha's opinion, is the greatest tragedy of Islam?

Kamran Pasha, "'Honor Killing' and Islam," HuffingtonPost.com, February 19, 2009. All rights reserved.
Reproduced by permission.

The American Muslim community is reeling this week [in February 2009] from news of the horrific beheading of Aasiya Hassan, allegedly by her husband Muzzammil Hassan. They were respected members of the community and co-founded BridgesTV, a television network ironically dedicated to fighting negative stereotypes of Muslims. As one of the first Muslims to succeed as a writer in Hollywood, I have been interviewed several times on BridgesTV and was delighted by the professionalism and media savvy of its staff. I had never met the Hassans, but I had been proud of their accomplishments. They were bringing an Islam of love, compassion and human brotherhood to the world, while countering the horrific images of violence and misogyny that had tainted how my fellow Americans saw my faith. The Hassans were people I admired—educated professionals and patriotic Americans with a commitment to family and community.

And then I heard how Aasiya Hassan died and I wanted to throw up.

This Is *Not* Islam

Right now there is a great deal of discussion in the media about whether her murder was an "honor killing." And among the more bigoted commentators, there are cries that this horrific murder has proven the "true face of Islam" to the world. That no matter how hard Muslims try to sell an Islam of peace and social justice, a headless corpse of a poor, abused woman will always be its legacy to humanity. I hear these words, and I want to cry out "No! This isn't Islam! This isn't the beautiful religion that brings comfort and joy to a billion people worldwide." But then I see images in my mind of Aasiya Hassan lying decapitated in a pool of blood and I am left wondering why anyone should listen.

The greatest tragedy for me as a Muslim is that my faith is associated with such horrific actions that run counter to everything that Prophet Muhammad stood for. To those who know little about Islamic history, it may sound laughable to assert that Islam began as a proto-feminist movement. But it's true. Perhaps the way out of this madness for the Muslim community is to look back at the life of Prophet Muhammad and remember his true legacy as a visionary champion of women's rights.

Islam Empowered Women in the Beginning

I recently finished my first novel, *Mother of the Believers*, which tells the story of Islam's birth from the perspective of Aisha, the Prophet's young wife. As a scholar, poet and warrior, Aisha was one of the most influential women in history, and her life reveals how empowered the women of Islam were at the onset of the faith. As I researched the story of early Islam for my novel, I was struck by how central [a role] women's rights played in the community's identity from the beginning. The Prophet was a sensitive man who had been orphaned at a young age and grew up in poverty. He saw from childhood the suffering of women and children in pre-Islamic Arabia, where the strong crushed the weak, and dedicated his life to changing the system.

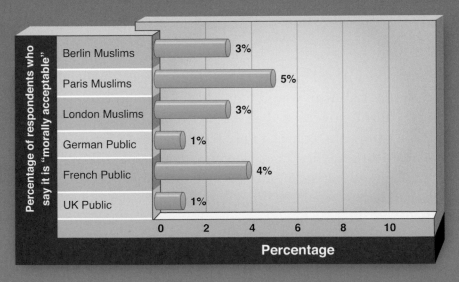

Muslims Are Just as Likely to Condemn Honor Killings as Other Groups

Muslims are sometimes portrayed as condoning honor killings, but a Gallup poll found that European and Muslim respondents in three European cities have similar views on this issue.

Question: "Are honor killings morally acceptable or morally wrong?"

Percentage of respondents who say it is "morally acceptable"

	Percentage
Berlin Muslims	3%
Paris Muslims	5%
London Muslims	3%
German Public	1%
French Public	4%
UK Public	1%

Percentage

Taken from: Gallup poll, May 28, 2008.

Honor killings occur in the United States. In 2011 Muzzammil Hassan (pictured) received a lengthy prison sentence for the brutal slaying of his wife, who had asked for a divorce.

One of the first Arab practices he outlawed was female infanticide. Pre-Islamic Arab men would bury alive unwanted baby girls in the desert, a horrific tradition that Prophet Muhammad ended forever. There is a powerful scene in the Holy Qur'an depicting Judgment Day where the souls of all girls who were slain would rise and confront their fathers, asking the men: "For what crime did you kill me?" And then their fathers would be flung into Hell. It is a vivid image meant to inculcate the true horror of such crimes in the minds of Arabs accustomed to centuries of brutal child murder.

The Prophet also established women's right to inherit and own property—rights that were not given to Christian women until the 19th century in Europe and America. Considering his concern for women's welfare, it is not surprising that the Prophet's earliest followers were female. The first Muslim was his wife Khadijah, a wealthy widow who had been his employer and had proposed marriage to the penniless Muhammad when he was managing her caravans. The first martyr of Islam, Sumaya, was an elderly woman who was killed by Meccan idolaters for refusing to renounce monotheism.

A Pre-Islamic Tradition Outlawed by Islam

So if all this is true, where does this idea of "honor killing" come from in the Muslim world? Unfortunately, it is one of the ugly elements of pre-Islamic Arabian culture that continues to reassert itself, despite the Prophet's efforts to eradicate the practice. In fact, Prophet Muhammad nearly lost his own beloved wife to the madness of the crowds screaming about "sexual honor." In my novel, I detail how his wife Aisha was once falsely accused of adultery and was the victim of a gossip campaign meant to destroy her reputation and potentially her life. The Holy Qur'an exonerated her of the false accusations, and then demanded that anyone accusing a woman of adultery would have to bring four witnesses to the act of sexual intercourse. Of course, such a requirement is impossible to meet, and its purpose was to end the threat to women's lives under claims of "preserving honor."

> **FAST FACT**
>
> Islam scholar John L. Esposito reports that honor killings are a largely cultural phenomenon. They occur in India, where victims are Christian, Hindu, and Sikh. Honor killings also occurred in many non-Islamic ancient civilizations, including Babylonia, biblical Israel, and Rome.

Aisha was saved, but generations of women continue to be haunted by this curse from The Days of Ignorance, as Muslims refer to the era before Islam. The greatest tragedy of Islam is that some Muslim men continue to uphold these pagan practices that the Prophet outlawed 1,400 years ago.

Bringing Disrepute to Islam

As a believer, I have no doubt that those who commit murder in the name of Islam will face the wrath of God in this life and in eternity. But personal belief is not enough. Islam is a religion of action. Muslim men must stand and fight against this evil of "honor killing" that destroys lives and families, shatters the bond of love between men and women, and brings disrepute to Islam, which was sent as a beacon of light to the world. If we fail to do so, we will have failed to follow the example of Prophet Muhammad, a kind and compassionate man who never struck a woman or child in his life. If we remain silent, we will have earned the cruel labels that Islamophobes and bigots seek to give us—barbarians, fanatics and monsters.

The choice that stands before Muslim men is stark. Do we follow ancient and evil practices, creating a cycle of violence and grief, and use culture as an excuse for our sins? Or do we follow our Prophet and create a better world where men and women treat each other with dignity and love? Do we turn life on this Earth into Hell, or into Paradise? The answer will reveal whether we are Muslims, people who have surrendered themselves to the true God of mercy and compassion, or idolaters, people who fashion God according to their own self-serving desires.

May God have mercy on the soul of Aasiya Hassan, and on her children and loved ones. May her tragic death serve as a catalyst to end this ancient and un-Islamic practice of "honor killing" forever.

EVALUATING THE AUTHOR'S ARGUMENTS:

"This is not Islam" is a common refrain heard from those, such as Kamran Pasha, who insist that violent and oppressive acts committed in Islam's name are not really Islamic. What do you think? What relationship do you think Islam has with these acts, if any? Quote from at least two authors in this chapter in your answer.

Chapter 3

What Is the Status of Islam and Muslims in the United States?

Islam's place in American politics and society is complicated, and still emerging.

Discrimination Against American Muslims Is a Serious Problem

John L. Esposito

"Hate crimes against Muslims are on the rise across the country."

In the following viewpoint John L. Esposito argues that "Islamophobia"—fear or hatred of Islam and Muslims—is an increasingly serious problem in America. He explains that there is a creeping acceptance of hate speech against Muslims, which has even been uttered by some of America's highest politicians. There has also been an upsurge in hate crimes against Muslim Americans, protests against their right to worship freely, and an increase in prejudice toward them among the general public. Esposito says that Muslim Americans are the latest in a long line of scapegoated groups—such as Jews or blacks—that have experienced discrimination and prejudice as a result of American fear and bigotry. He argues that when one group is discriminated against, the rights of all Americans come under threat. He urges the media to stop reporting sensationalized or misleading stories that paint Muslims in a bad light and for the general public to realize that hate speech and behavior hurts the whole of society.

Esposito is a widely respected scholar and professor of Islamic studies. He is the founding director of the Centre for Muslim-Christian Understanding. He is also coauthor of *Who Speaks for Islam? What a Billion Muslims Really Think,* and author of the book *The Future of Islam.*

AS YOU READ, CONSIDER THE FOLLOWING QUESTIONS:
1. What does Esposito say that placards carried by Christians who protested a mosque in Bridgeport, Connecticut, read?
2. What is meant by the phrase "what bleeds, leads" as used by the author?
3. What percentage of Americans does Esposito say admit to feeling at least a little prejudiced toward Muslims?

There is no lack of hate speech in the media and in print to empower Islamophobia. The primary focus is often not balanced reporting, or even coverage of positive news about Muslims but on highlighting acts and statements of political and religious extremists. And hate crimes against Muslims are on the rise across the United States.

We are passing through difficult and dangerous times. The impact of staggering economic crisis and fears of a continued terrorist threat have spawned a culture of hate that threatens the future of our American way of life and values.

Islamophobia Is the New Way to Hate

The legacy of the 9/11 and post-9/11 terrorist attacks has been exploited by media commentators, hard-line Christian Zionists and political candidates whose fear-mongering targets Islam and Muslims. Islamophobia is fast becoming for Muslims what anti-Semitism is for Jews. Rooted in hostility and intolerance towards religious and cultural beliefs and a religious or racial group, it threatens the democratic fabric of American and European societies. Like anti-Semites and

When asked their feelings toward four religious groups, Americans are more likely to express bias toward Muslims than members of other faiths.

Question: "Thinking honestly about your feelings, how much prejudice, if any, do you feel toward each of the following religious groups?"

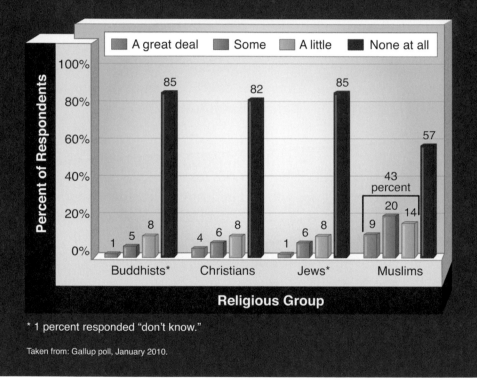

* 1 percent responded "don't know."

Taken from: Gallup poll, January 2010.

racists, Islamophobes are the first to protest that their stereotyping and scapegoating of these "others" as a threat to all of us, incapable of integration or loyalty, are not Islamophobic. Yet, examples that illustrate the social cancer of Islamophobia that is spreading across the United States, infringing upon the constitutional rights of American citizens, abound:

Across the U.S. a major debate has erupted over building an Islamic community center a few blocks from the site of the World Trade

Center. Amidst the voices opposing this venture, even the ADL [Anti-Defamation League] (the organization devoted to fighting defamation and prejudice) decided to oppose the building, not because Muslims do not have a right to build the center but rather to protect the feelings of those opposed! Is this a criterion the ADL has used or would subscribe to in its own struggles against anti-Semitism? The ADL's position contrasted sharply with that of J Street [in Washington, DC, where many Jewish and pro-Israel lobbying groups are located], rabbis and Jewish activists.

Today, opposition to mosque construction with claims that all mosques are "monuments to terrorism" and "house embedded [terrorist] cells" in locations from NYC [New York City] and Staten Island [New York], to Tennessee and California, has become not just a local but a national political issue.

Anti-Muslim Rhetoric and Action Abound

In California, a Tea Party Rally to protest an Islamic Center in Temecula, encouraged protesters to bring their dogs because Muslims allegedly hate Jews, Christians, women, and dogs.

Christians from a right-wing church in Dallas, Texas, traveled to a Bridgeport, Conn., mosque to confront worshippers. These Christians shouted "Murderers!" at the young children leaving the mosque. Carrying placards, they angrily declared "Islam is a lie," . . . "Jesus hates Muslims" . . . "This is a war in America and we are taking it to the mosques around the country."

Politicians use fear of Islam as a political football. [Former House Speaker and 2012 presidential candidate] Newt Gingrich warned of the danger of shariah [Islamic law] taking over American courts. Republican [state senator] Rex Duncan of Oklahoma, declared there is a "war for the survival of America," to keep the shariah from creeping into the American court system. Even the new [Supreme Court] Justice [Elena] Kagan is being accused of being "Justice Shariah."

Congresswoman Sue Myrick from NC [North Carolina] and Congressman Paul Broun from Georgia recklessly charged that Muslim student interns were part of a secret infiltration of Muslim spies into key national security committees on Capitol Hill.

Hate crimes against Muslims are on the rise across the country.

The Essence of Islamophobia

What constitutes an Islamophobe? Islamophobes believe that:

- Islam, not just a small minority of extremists and terrorists, is the problem and a threat to the West.
- The religion of Islam has no common values with the West.
- Islam and Muslims are inferior to Judaism and Christianity.
- Islam is an inherently violent religion and political ideology rather than a source of faith and spirituality.
- Muslims cannot integrate and become loyal citizens.
- Most mosques should be monitored for embedded cells.
- Islam encourages its followers to launch a global jihad against all non-Muslims but in particular against the West.

Hurtful Stereotypes and Misrepresentations

There is no lack of hate speech in the media and in print to empower Islamophobia. The media, whose primary driver is sales and circulations, caters to explosive, headline events:

"What bleeds, leads." The primary focus is often not balanced reporting, or even coverage of positive news about Muslims but on highlighting acts and statements of political and religious extremists. Political and religious commentators write and speak out publicly about Islam and Muslims, asserting with impunity what would never appear in mainstream broadcast or print media about Jews, Christians and other established ethnic groups. If one takes out the word "Muslim" and substitutes "Jew" or "Catholic" in many of the articles targeting Muslims, the negative public reaction would be monumental.

> **FAST FACT**
>
> An August 2011 Gallup poll found that 48 percent of Muslim Americans have experienced religious or racial discrimination during the past year. This is more than twice as many as other religious groups, except for Mormons (31 percent).

The net result? All Muslims have been reduced to stereotypes of Islam against the West, Islam's war with modernity, and Muslim rage, extremism, fanaticism, and terrorism. The rhetoric and hatred

Protesters in New York City demonstrate against the proposed construction of an Islamic mosque and community center near the World Trade Center site.

of a violent minority has been equated with the "Anti-Americanism or anti-Westernism of a peaceful, mainstream majority, all lumped together in the question (more a belief) "Why do they hate us?" Islam and Muslims, not just the small minority of Muslim extremists and terrorists, are cast as the peculiar and demonized "other" with serious international and domestic consequences.

Americans Think Poorly of Muslims

In the Gallup World Poll, when U.S. respondents were asked what they admire about the Muslim world, the most common response was "nothing" (33 percent); the second most common was "I don't know" (22 percent). Despite major polling by Gallup and PEW that show that American Muslims are well integrated economically and politically, a January 2010 Gallup Center for Muslim Studies report found that more than 4 in 10 Americans (43%) admit to feeling at least "a little" prejudice toward Muslims—more than twice the number who say the same about Christians (18%), Jews (15%) and Buddhists (14%). Nine percent of Americans admitted feeling "a great deal" of prejudice towards Muslims, while 20% admitted feeling "some" prejudice. Surprisingly, Gallup data revealed a link between anti-Semitism and Islamophobia, that contempt for Jews makes a person "about 32 times as likely to report the same level of prejudice toward Muslims."

Islamophobia, like anti-Semitism, will not be eradicated easily or soon. We all (governments, policymakers, the media, educational institutions, religious and corporate leaders) have a critical role to play in countering the voices of hate, the exclusivist theologies and ideologies. Islamophobic campaigns force even the most moderate and open-minded Muslims to question the value of integrating into the larger society when the leaders of that society look at all Muslims with suspicion and prejudice. This is not reconcilable either with Judeo-Christian ethics or the civic moral values of America and Europe.

A Threat to All Americans

Attempts to limit public discourse and debate, to silence alternative voices speaking out against ignorance, stereotyping and demonization of Islam, discrimination, hate crimes or threats to the civil liberties of Muslims must be turned back if America is to be preserved as the country of unity in diversity and free speech and opportunity for all. Education in our schools and universities and seminaries (as well as our churches and synagogues) that train the next generation of policymakers, religious leaders, educators, and citizens will be critical. What is at stake is the very core of who and what we are as a nation and a society, the foundation of our identity. Islamophobia and its culture of hate is not only a threat to the civil liberties of Muslims but also the very fabric of who we are and what we stand for, the principles and values embodied in our constitution and which have historically made our democracy strong.

EVALUATING THE AUTHORS' ARGUMENTS:

How do you think John L. Esposito would respond to the following viewpoint by Jeff Jacoby that argues that discrimination against Muslim Americans is not a serious problem because they have not been the victim of the majority of hate crimes. Write at least two to three sentences on what you think he might say. Then, state with which author you agree—is discrimination against Muslim Americans a serious problem? Why or why not? What piece of evidence helped you come to this conclusion?

Viewpoint 2

Discrimination Against American Muslims Has Been Exaggerated

"For American Muslims . . . tension and hostility are the exception. America's exemplary tolerance is the rule."

Jeff Jacoby

Jeff Jacoby is a columnist for the *Boston Globe.* In the following viewpoint he argues that "Islamophobia"—the discrimination against and fear and hatred of Muslim Americans—has been exaggerated and is largely untrue. He discusses statistics compiled by law enforcement agencies, including the FBI, that show Muslims are victims in fewer than 10 percent of all hate crimes. When Muslims are targeted, Jacoby says the behavior is loudly condemned by Christian, Jewish, and secular groups. Jacoby contends that, on the whole, America is a safe and tolerant place for Muslims. Hostility against them is rare, though he admits that at least some conflict is to be expected considering that America is at war with violent extremists who claim to act in Islam's name. Jacoby concludes that the vast majority of American Muslims enjoy safety, freedom, and equality and that the problem of Islamophobia in America is largely a myth.

AS YOU READ, CONSIDER THE FOLLOWING QUESTIONS:
1. How many mosques are there in the United States today compared with in 2001, according to Jacoby?
2. According to polls cited by Jacoby, in what nation do Muslims say they feel the most free and safe?
3. What percentage of hate crimes in 2009 were committed against Muslims and what percentage against Jews, as reported by the author?

"Is America Islamophobic?"

When that provocative question appeared on the cover of *Time* in August [2010], the accompanying story strained to imply, on the basis of some anecdotal evidence, that the answer might be yes. The FBI's latest compendium of US hate-crimes data suggests far more plausibly that the answer is no.

Not a Serious Problem

"Where ordinary Americans meet Islam, there is evidence that suspicion and hostility are growing," the *Time* article said. "To be a Muslim in America now is to endure slings and arrows against your faith— not just in the schoolyard and the office but also outside your place of worship and in the public square, where some of the country's most powerful mainstream religious and political leaders unthinkingly (or worse, deliberately) conflate Islam with terrorism and savagery."

Time published that article amid the tumult over plans to build a Muslim mosque and cultural center near Ground Zero in New York,

FAST FACT

A 2010 poll by the Pew Research Center found that the majority of Americans—62 percent— believe Muslims should have the same rights as other religious groups to build houses of worship in local communities.

In 2010 Chicago Muslims pray during Eid-ul-Fitr services marking the end of Ramadan. They were joined by many Christian and Jewish religious leaders in a show of support for the Islamic community.

and not long after a fringe pastor in Gainesville [Texas] had announced that he intended to burn copies of the Koran on the anniversary of the 9/11 attacks. The piece noted that a handful of other mosque projects nationwide have run into "bitter opposition," and it cited a Duke University professor's claim that such resistance is "part of a pattern of intolerance" against American Muslims. Yet the story conceded frankly that "there's no sign that violence against Muslims is on the rise" and that "Islamophobia in the US doesn't approach levels seen in other countries."

In fact, as *Time* pointed out, while there may be the occasional confrontation over a Muslim construction project, "there are now 1,900 mosques in the US, up from about 1,200 in 2001." Even after 9/11, in other words, and even as radical Islamists continue to target Americans, places of worship for Muslims in the United States have proliferated. And whenever naked anti-Islamic bigotry has appeared, "it has been denounced by many Christian, Jewish, and secular groups."

More Hate Crimes Against Jews

America is many things, but "Islamophobic" plainly isn't one of them. As *Time* itself acknowledged: "Polls have shown that most Muslims feel safer and freer in the US than anywhere else in the Western world." That sentiment is powerfully buttressed by the FBI's newly released statistics on hate crimes in the United States.

In 2009, according to data gathered from more than 14,000 law enforcement agencies nationwide, there were 1,376 hate crimes motivated by religious bias. Of those, just 9.3 percent—fewer than 1 in 10—were committed against Muslims. By contrast, 70.1 percent were committed against Jews, 6.9 percent were aimed at Catholics or Protestants, and 8.6 percent targeted other religions. Hate crimes driven by anti-Muslim bigotry were outnumbered nearly 8 to 1 by anti-Semitic crimes.

Year after year, American Jews are far more likely to be the victims of religious hate crime than members of any other group. That was true even in 2001, by far the worst year for anti-Muslim incidents, when 481 were reported—less than half of the 1,042 anti-Jewish crimes tabulated by the FBI the same year.

Most Americans Are Very Tolerant

Does all this mean that America is in reality a hotbed of anti-Semitism? Would *Time*'s cover have been closer to the mark if it had asked: "Is America Judeophobic?"

Of course not. Even one hate crime is one too many, but in a nation of 300 million, all of the religious-based hate crimes added together amount to less than a drop in the bucket. This is not to minimize the 964 hate crimes perpetrated against Jews last year, or those carried out against Muslims (128), Catholics (55), or Protestants (40). Some of those attacks were especially shocking or destructive; all of them should be punished. But surely the most obvious takeaway from the

Muslims Are Victims in the Minority of Hate Crimes

Statistics from the US Department of Justice show that in 2009 there were 8,336 victims of hate crimes. Of these crimes, 1,575 were anti-religious in nature, and of these, Muslim victims were the minority. The vast majority of hate crimes are committed against Jews, not Muslims.

Of the 1,575 victims of an antireligious hate crime:

- 71.9 percent were victims of an offender's anti-Jewish bias.

- 8.4 percent were victims because of an anti-Islamic bias.

- 3.7 percent were victims because of an anti-Catholic bias.

- 2.7 percent were victims because of an anti-Protestant bias.

- 0.7 percent were victims because of an anti-Atheist/Agnostic bias.

- 8.3 percent were victims because of a bias against other religions (anti–other religion)

- 4.3 percent were victims because of a bias against groups of individuals of varying religions (anti–multiple religious groups).

Taken from: Uniform Crime Report, Department of Justice. "Hate Crime Statistics, 2009," November 2010. www2.fbi.gov/ucr/hc2009/documents/victims.pdf.

FBI's statistics is not that anti-religious hate crimes are so frequent in America. It is that they are so rare.

In a column a few years back, I wrote that America has been for the Jews "a safe harbor virtually without parallel." It has proved much the same for Muslims. Of course there is tension and hostility sometimes. How could there not be, when America is at war with violent jihadists who have done so much harm in the name of Islam? But for American Muslims as for American Jews, the tension and hostility are the exception. America's exemplary tolerance is the rule.

Jeff Jacoby and John L. Esposito (author of the previous viewpoint) disagree with each other over whether "Islamophobia" is a serious problem in America. In your opinion, which author made the better argument? Why? List at least four pieces of evidence (quotes, statistics, facts, or statements of reasoning) that caused you to side with one author over the other.

Islamic Law Threatens America

"Under successive presidencies, the United States has failed to understand, let alone counter successfully, the threat posed to its constitutional form of government and free society by shariah."

Connie Hair

In the following viewpoint Connie Hair argues that Islamic law, or shariah, is incompatible with the US Constitution and threatens the American way of life. Hair uses a recent report entitled *Shariah: The Threat to America,* released by "a group of highly respected national security professionals," to illustrate how shariah has covertly permeated our government institutions. The report states that shariah is a doctrine of submission to Allah that governs all aspects of society. For this reason, Hair asserts, shariah law is at odds with America's core values of freedom of expression, economic liberty, freedom of conscience, privacy, and other key values. *Shariah: The Threat to America* concludes by recommending that US policy makers, as well as the public at large, resist efforts to allow shariah in America as an alternative to the laws and Constitution of the United States.

Connie Hair writes a weekly column for *Human Events.* She is a former speechwriter for Rep. Trent Franks (R-Ariz.).

AS YOU READ, CONSIDER THE FOLLOWING QUESTIONS:
  1. According to the viewpoint, what is "Team B II"?
  2. Why, according to the authors of *Shariah: The Threat to America,* is Islam a "political-military-legal doctrine" and not a religion?
  3. Name two reasons provided by the viewpoint as to why shariah law is not compatible with the US Constitution.

A group of highly respected national security professionals dubbed "Team B II" are releasing a major new study today [September 15, 2010] of the threat America faces from Islamic shariah law currently creeping into our legal system.

Shariah: The Threat to America

Human Events got an advance look at the document. The report, entitled "Shariah: The Threat to America" . . . takes a fresh look at shariah law, placing vital information in the hands of average, everyday Americans and intelligence officials alike and offers a chilling threat assessment of shariah's crushing incompatibility with the U.S. Constitution.

The report is being released today at a Capitol Hill press conference by members of the "Team B II" threat assessment team. Those team members include former Deputy Under Secretary of Defense for Intelligence Lieutenant General William G. "Jerry" Boykin, former Assistant U.S. Attorney Andrew C. McCarthy and Center for Security Policy President Frank Gaffney.

During the Cold War with Soviet Russia, analysis from the CIA and other intelligence agencies had missed the mark by basing threat assessments on input from policymakers, not on actual, factual threat doctrine. In 1976, "Team B" was formed to take a more thorough, realistic look at the enemy.

This study from highly respected, top intelligence and policy experts is the result of months of analysis, discussion and drafting and focuses on the preeminent totalitarian threat of our time: the legal-political-military doctrine known within Islam as shariah.

The analysis provides a comprehensive "second opinion" to official U.S. government assessments and characterizations of the shariah threat.

Muslim extremists demonstrate in London. These proponents of sharia law want the laws of Islam to supersede democracy.

It offers examples from history and from widely accepted sources of authority in the Islamic community to present the unfiltered nature of shariah law, challenging today's assumptions euphemistically described as "violent extremism"—as well as the policies of co-existence, accommodation and submission that are rooted in those assumptions.

A sample from the report:

Tolerance in America Versus the Quran

"This brief examination of American principles establishes that American principles are principles of liberty are rooted in mutual toleration. It follows that, in the United States, liberty [and] was never intended to tolerate the intolerant and its citizens were never intended to tolerate totalitarian doctrines. Put differently, intolerant, totalitarian doctrines are in direct conflict with the stated purpose of American government 'to secure these rights [endowed by their Creator].'

"Even a fairly superficial reading of the Quran and other primary source documents of shariah reveals that it is a political-military-legal

doctrine, rather than a religion as defined by the American standards mentioned above. The prominent Islamic scholar Abdul Mawdudi concurs with this assessment, saying: 'But the truth is that Islam is not the name of a "Religion," nor is "Muslim" the title of a "Nation." In reality, Islam is a revolutionary ideology and program which seeks to alter the social order of the whole world and rebuild it in conformity with its own tenets and ideals.'

"*Shariah is, moreover, a doctrine that mandates the rule of Allah over all aspects of society. Specifically, in contrast—and fundamentally at odds— with the Virginia Statute for Religious Liberty, shariah holds that God did not create the mind free, but in subservience to the will of Allah (as detailed in shariah). The condition of human beings is submission to Allah, not freedom.*"

From submission, dhimmitude and shariah blasphemy codes to "fear as reason" policy, this analysis offers a stunning look at what "moderates" and "violent extremists" alike desire—including so-called "moderates" like Ground Zero mosque Imam Feisal Abdul Rauf.

They seek an America that is "shariah compliant."

The True Character of Shariah

Conclusions offered in the report are an eye-opener. Another sampling:

"*Under successive presidencies, the United States has failed to understand, let alone counter successfully, the threat posed to its constitutional form of government and free society by shariah. In the past, such failures were reckless. Today, they are intolerable.*

"*The preceding pages document shariah's true supremacist and totalitarian character. They make clear its incompatibility with the Constitution as the only source of law for this country. As we have* seen, shariah explicitly seeks to replace representative governance with an Islamic state, to destroy sovereign and national polities with a global caliphate.

"If shariah is thus viewed as an alien legal system hostile to and in contravention of the U.S. Constitution, and as one which dictates both violent and non-violent means to a capable audience ready to act imminently, then logically, those who seek to establish shariah in America—whether by violent means or by stealth—can be said to be engaged in criminal sedition, not the protected practice of a religion."

Recommendations by "Team B II"

And a further sampling of the recommendations in the report reflect the seriousness of the threat we face from an ideology that has covertly permeated our government institutions.

"While detailed recommendations for adopting a more prudential and effective strategy for surviving shariah's onslaught are beyond the scope of this study, several policy and programmatic changes are clearly in order. These include:

- U.S. policy-makers, financiers, businessmen, judges, journalists, community leaders and the public at large must be equipped with an accurate understanding of the nature of shariah and the necessity of keeping America shariah-free. At a minimum, this will entail resisting—rather than acquiescing to—the concerted efforts now being made to allow that alien and barbaric legal code to become established in this country as an alternate, parallel system to the Constitution and the laws enacted pursuant to it. Arguably, this is already in effect for those who have taken an oath to 'support and defend' the Constitution, because the requirement is subsumed in that oath.
- U.S. government agencies and organizations should cease their outreach to Muslim communities through Muslim Brotherhood fronts whose mission is to destroy our country from within as such practices are both reckless and counterproductive. Indeed, these activities serve to legitimate, protect and expand the influence of our enemies. They conduce to no successful legal outcome that cannot be better advanced via aggressive prosecution of terrorists, terror-funders and other lawbreakers. It also discourages patriotic

Americans Do Not Think Muslim Americans Are Treated Unfairly Because of Their Religion

The majority of Americans do not think Muslim Americans are treated unfairly because of their religion.

Question: "Are most American Muslims living in the United States treated unfairly because of their religion and ethnicity?"

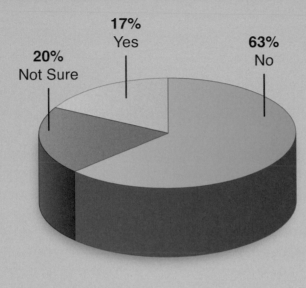

20%
Not Sure

17%
Yes

63%
No

Taken from: Rasmussen Reports, March 11, 2011.

Muslims from providing actual assistance to the U.S. government lest they be marked for ostracism or worse by the Brothers and other shariah-adherent members of their communities.

- In keeping with Article VI of the Constitution, extend bans currently in effect that bar members of hate groups such as the Ku Klux Klan from holding positions of trust in federal, state, or local governments or the armed forces of the United States to those who espouse or support shariah. Instead, every effort should be made to identify and empower Muslims who are willing publicly to denounce shariah.

- Practices that promote shariah—notably, shariah-compliant finance and the establishment or promotion in public spaces or with public funds of facilities and activities that give preferential treatment to shariah's adherents—are incompatible with the Constitution and the freedoms it enshrines and must be proscribed.

• Sedition is prohibited by law in the United States. To the extent that imams [Muslim prayer leaders] and mosques are being used to advocate shariah in America, they are promoting seditious activity and should be warned that they will not be immune from prosecution."

EVALUATING THE AUTHORS' ARGUMENTS:

Connie Hair warns that shariah law is a threatening ideology that challenges the fundamental beliefs and values of the United States. Reza Aslan, author of the following viewpoint, argues it is irrational to fear that Islamic law might dominate American institutions or communities. After reading both viewpoints, with which author do you agree? Do you think shariah law should be feared and banned? Why or why not? Quote from the texts you have read in your answer.

It Is Irrational to Think Islamic Law Will Take Over America

Reza Aslan

"We [Muslims] will need to raise our numbers from the 1 percent of the US population we currently represent, to at least 2 percent before we can begin stoning people at random."

Calls to ban Islamic law, or shariah, in the United States are ridiculous and irrational, argues Reza Aslan in the following viewpoint. He discusses the attempt of several conservative politicians to ban Islamic law from being used as a source of jurisprudence in American courts. Aslan says that sharia has never been used as the basis for any court case, so it seems unnecessary to ban it. Furthermore, Muslim organizations have not tried to impose Islamic law on any community or institution, and Islamic law has not been adopted anywhere in the United States. Aslan says Muslims make up such a small minority of Americans, it is laughable to think they could or would seek to dominate American institutions with their religious laws. He concludes that efforts to ban Islamic law are part of the irrational wave of anti-Muslim hysteria sweeping the United States.

Aslan is a Muslim American and the editor of the political news website The Daily Beast. He is also the author of the books *No God but God* and *Tablet and Pen: Literary Landscapes from the Modern Middle East*.

AS YOU READ, CONSIDER THE FOLLOWING QUESTIONS:
1. Who is Sharron Angle as mentioned by the author?
2. What kind of amendment did Oklahoma state senator Rex Duncan introduce in 2010, according to Aslan?
3. What product does writer Robert Spencer warn is evidence of the Muslim takeover of America, in the author's opinion?

We all knew Nevada's Republican Senatorial candidate Sharron Angle was a bit loony. After all, this is the woman who said that rape and incest victims who become pregnant should be forced to have their babies so as to turn their "lemon situation into lemonade."

But when Angle suggested last week [in October 2010] that certain American cities like Dearborn, Michigan and Frankford, Texas, have been taken over by a "militant terrorist situation" wherein Muslims have instituted Sharia law upon its residents, many people were left scratching their heads at what she could possibly have meant.

No Reason for Hysteria Over Islamic Law

It's not just that Dearborn is—last anyone checked—still under the purview of the United States Constitution, or that there is no place in America called Frankford, Texas (I'm not kidding, look it up). It's the rather bizarre notion that there may be a city in this country where the Constitution does not apply. "It seems to me there is something fundamentally wrong with allowing a foreign system of law to even take hold in any municipality or government situation in our United States," Angle said about the real Dearborn and the imaginary Frankford.

Angle is right. There is something fundamentally wrong with this idea—it's not true. There is no city or municipality in this country where Islamic law has taken hold. And yet, Angle is not the only one sounding the alarm over an imminent Muslim takeover of America.

Indeed, now that the screeching over the building of the Islamic Community Center in Lower Manhattan seems to have died down, a new battle cry is arising from the radical anti-Muslim fringe: American Muslims, they say, are trying to replace the Constitution with Sharia!

A Ridiculous Idea

Now I admit that we Muslims are a pretty powerful bunch. But in all the secret Muslim gatherings I have attended to discuss our plans for destroying democracy and taking over the White House (we meet every Friday night directly atop Ground Zero), we have come to the conclusion that we will need to raise our numbers from the 1% of the US population we currently represent, to at least 2% before we can begin stoning people at random.

Still, it's good to know there are God-fearing Americans like Oklahoma State Senator Rex Duncan who are taking steps to prevent such an outcome. Citing a need to protect the American constitution from the "looming threat" of Muslims, Duncan has introduced an amendment outlawing Sharia from Oklahoma's court system. Duncan admits that his measure, which Oklahomans will vote on

According to the author, anti-sharia law proponent Pamela Geller (pictured) is the most strident voice among those who believe that Muslims are taking over America.

this fall,[1] may be a bit premature. After all, there are only about 30,000 Muslims in the entire state. But he's not taking any chances. "I see [sharia] in the future somewhere in America," Duncan said. "It's not an imminent threat in Oklahoma yet, but it's a storm on the horizon in other states" (By *other states* I believe Duncan is referring to Frankford, Texas).

So Loud, So Hysterical

The loudest and most hysterical voice among the Muslims-are-taking-over-America chorus belongs to the pseudo-scholar and professional noise-maker Robert Spencer [of the website jihadwatch.org] who, along with Pamela Geller—most famous for her theory that [President Barack] Obama is Malcom X's bastard Muslim love-child—formed the organization behind the anti-mosque protests that have erupted all over the country. Spencer is convinced that Sharia has begun to take over the American legal system. His proof? The new Supreme Court justice Elena Kagan.

In an interview with the conservative website The Daily Caller, Spencer claimed that Kagan "would knowingly and wittingly abet the advance of Sharia," in her tenure as Supreme Court justice because, as a liberal, she shares with Muslims "a hatred of the West and Western civilization." Now, Spencer also believes that the decision by Campbell Soup to create a line of halal soups to accompany its kosher line is another sign of the Muslim takeover of America ("why is Campbell's Soup rushing to do [Muslims'] bidding?" Spencer wrote in his blog. "M-M-Muslim Brotherhood Good?"), so he is obviously a nut who should not be taken seriously on any subject.

FAST FACT

There are about 2.6 million Muslims living in the United States—less than 1 percent of the total population.

But then how to explain [former House Speaker and 2012 presidential hopeful] Newt Gingrich? Fresh off his most recent media blitz, during which he compared Islam to Nazism and associated American Muslims with al-Qaeda terrorists, Gingrich

1. Oklahoma voters approved this amendment in November 2010, but it has since been blocked by courts.

States Are Moving to Ban Sharia Law from Being Used in Courts

According to the National Conference of State Legislatures, as of August 2011, sixteen states had introduced legislation to prevent courts from using foreign or religious law in their decisions.

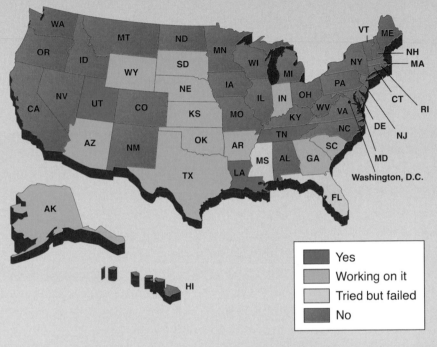

Taken from: Tim Murphy. "Map: Has Your State Banned Sharia?" Motherjones.com, February 11, 2011.

has enthusiastically taken up the anti-Muslim cause. He recently released a film titled "America at Risk," which details the Muslim threat to America ("This is the end of times," the film warns. "This is the final struggle"). Now he is calling for a federal law banning Sharia in the U.S.

"We should have a federal law that says Sharia law cannot be recognized by any court in the United States," Gingrich told an audience at the Values Voter Summit in D.C. last month [September 2010]. He wants the law to stipulate that, "no judge will remain in office [who] tried to use Sharia law."

Banning Sharia Is Like Banning Unicorns

Considering that no judge in the United States has cited Sharia in any legal case, and that no Muslim organization has called for its imposition in America, this is a bit like passing a federal law banning Americans from riding unicorns. Yet it does bear mentioning that there are already a number of religious courts all over this country through which a particular religious community can adjudicate matters of family law for themselves. They are called Halacha (Jewish law) courts and they allow observant Jews to conduct business and personal transactions in accordance with the principles of the Torah as long as Halacha does not violate the civil law. Why shouldn't Muslims in the US have the same opportunity as America's Jews when it comes to issues of marriage, divorce, and inheritance.

As Marc Stern, associate counsel for the American Jewish Committee, put it in an interview with NPR [National Public Radio]: "Just as the Catholic Church . . . didn't take over [constitutional] law when large numbers of Catholics came to the United States, and Jewish law doesn't govern Jewish citizens [of the United States], Shariah law is not going to govern, except voluntarily, the rights and responsibilities of Muslim citizens in the United States."

But these are just facts and, as such, have no bearing on the non-sense pouring out of the mouths of the Sharron Angles and Robert Spencers of the world. So while they continue with this newest round of their fear Islam campaign, I, for one, am going to move to Frankford, Texas where I can finally marry four wives.

EVALUATING THE AUTHOR'S ARGUMENTS:

Reza Aslan uses humor and sarcasm to make his point that it is irrational to fear a Muslim takeover of the United States. Identify all instances in which he uses humor or sarcasm—you can make a list of them or highlight their use in the text. Then, explain whether or not they helped convince you of the author's argument. Did you find humor and sarcasm to be effective vehicles for arguing his point? Why or why not?

Facts About Islam

Editor's note: These facts can be used in reports or papers to reinforce or add credibility when making important points or claims.

Islam Around the World

According to the *CIA World Factbook*, as of August 2011 there were fifty-five predominantly Muslim countries or territories:

1. Afghanistan
2. Albania
3. Algeria
4. Azerbaijan
5. Bahrain
6. Bangladesh
7. Bosnia and Herzegovina
8. Brunei
9. Burkina Faso
10. Chad
11. Cocos (Keeling) Islands
12. Comoros
13. Cote d'Ivoire
14. Djibouti
15. Egypt
16. Eritrea
17. The Gambia
18. Gaza Strip
19. Guinea
20. Guinea-Bissau
21. Indonesia
22. Iran
23. Iraq
24. Jordan
25. Kazakhstan
26. Kosovo
27. Kuwait
28. Kyrgyzstan
29. Lebanon
30. Libya
31. Malaysia
32. Maldives
33. Mali
34. Mauritania
35. Morocco
36. Niger
37. Nigeria
38. Oman
39. Pakistan
40. Qatar
41. Saudi Arabia
42. Senegal
43. Sierra Leone
44. Somalia
45. Sudan
46. Syria
47. Tajikistan
48. Tunisia
49. Turkey
50. Turkmenistan
51. United Arab Emirates
52. Uzbekistan
53. West Bank
54. Western Sahara
55. Yemen

According to the *CIA World Factbook:*
- Islam is the world's second-largest religion.
- Islam is the world's fastest-growing religion.
- About 23 percent of the world's total population is Muslim. That is more than 1 in 5 people on the planet.
- About 75 percent of the world's Muslims identify with the majority Muslim sect, Sunni.
- About 10–20 percent are Shiite, a minority sect.

The five countries with the largest populations of Muslims are:
- Indonesia (213 million Muslims)
- Pakistan (156 million Muslims)
- India (138 million Muslims)
- Bangladesh (127 million Muslims)
- Egypt (70 million Muslims)

In fourteen countries, at least 99 percent of the population is Muslim. These are:
- Saudi Arabia (100 percent)
- Somalia (100 percent)
- Mauritania (99.9 percent)
- Maldives (99.9 percent)
- Western Sahara (99.8 percent)
- Comoros (99 percent)
- Tunisia (99 percent)
- Yemen (99 percent)
- Djibouti (99 percent)
- Afghanistan (99 percent)
- Oman (99 percent)
- Algeria (99 percent)
- Turkey (99 percent)
- Iran (99 percent)

According to a 2011 study by the Pew Research Center's Forum on Religion and Public Life:
- The world's Muslim population will increase by about 35 percent by 2030.
- There were 1.6 billion Muslims worldwide in 2010; there will be about 2.2 billion worldwide by 2030.

- The global Muslim population will grow at about twice the rate as the non-Muslim population in that period.
- By 2030 Muslims will make up 26.4 percent of the world's total projected population of 8.3 billion by 2030.
- In 2010 seventy-two countries had a million or more Muslim inhabitants.
- By 2030 seventy-nine countries will have a million or more Muslim inhabitants.

Islam in Europe

According to the BBC (British Broadcasting Corporation), Islam is the fastest-growing religion in Europe, the result of immigration and high birthrates.

According to a 2011 study by the Pew Research Center's Forum on Religion and Public Life:
- In 2010 there were about 44.1 million Muslims in Europe.
- By 2030 there are expected to be about 58.5 million Muslims in Europe, a 31.9 percent increase.
- Between 1990 and 2010 Europe's Muslim population increased by almost 50 percent.
- In 1990 Muslims made up about 4.1 percent of Europe's total population.
- In 2010 Muslims made up about 6 percent of Europe's total population.
- By 2030 Muslims are expected to make up about 8 percent of Europe's total population.
- By 2030 Britain's Muslim population is expected to increase from 2.9 million to about 5.6 million, a 93 percent increase.
- By 2030 France's Muslim population is expected to increase from 4.7 million to about 6.9 million, a 46 percent increase. Muslims will compose about 10.3 percent of the French population.

Islam in the United States

According to a 2011 study by the Pew Research Center's Forum on Religion and Public Life:
- In 2010 Muslims composed about 0.8 percent of the American population.

- By 2030 they are expected to compose about 1.7 percent of the American population.
- In 2010 there were about 2.6 million Muslims in the United States.
- By 2030 the US Muslim population is expected to more than double, to about 6.2 million.

Opinions and Attitudes About Islam

A 2010 poll by *Newsweek* found that 41 percent of Americans personally know someone who is Muslim; 58 percent do not.

A 2010 poll by the Pew Research Center asked Americans how much they knew about Islam and its practices (numbers do not add up to 100 percent due to rounding):
- 9 percent said "a great deal."
- 35 percent said "some."
- 30 percent said "not very much."
- 25 percent said "nothing."

A 2011 poll by *USA Today* and the Gallup organization found the following about American opinions concerning Islam and Muslims (numbers for each topic may not add up to 100 percent due to rounding):
- 82 percent of Americans surveyed believe Muslims are committed to their religious beliefs.
- 8 percent said Muslims are not.
- 11 percent said they were unsure.

- 53 percent of Americans surveyed believe Muslims are supportive of the United States.
- 30 percent said they are not.
- 15 percent were unsure.

- 36 percent of Americans surveyed believe Muslims are too extreme in their religious beliefs.
- 50 percent said they are not.
- 15 percent said they were unsure.

- 28 percent of Americans surveyed believe Muslims are supportive of the terrorist group al Qaeda.
- 54 percent said they are not.
- 18 percent were unsure.

A 2011 Pew Research Center poll of Muslim Americans found the following about Muslim American beliefs, compared with other American religious groups:
- Muslim Americans are more likely to disapprove of military action against civilians:
  - 78 percent of Muslim Americans think that military action that targets and kills civilians is never justified.
  - 64 percent of Mormons, 58 percent of Protestants, 58 percent of Catholics, and 52 percent of Jews thought this.
- Muslim Americans are more likely to disapprove of terrorist activity:
  - 89 percent of Muslim Americans think it is never justified for an individual or small group of people to target and kill civilians.
  - 79 percent of Mormons, 75 percent of Jews, 71 percent of Catholics, and 71 percent of Protestants thought this.
- Muslim Americans are also:
  - less likely than other religious groups to have confidence in the military;
  - more likely to think that the wars in Iraq and Afghanistan were mistakes;
  - the religious group most skeptical of federal law enforcement;
  - and the most likely to say they have experienced racial or religious discrimination in the last year.
- 92 percent of Muslim Americans say Muslim Americans do not sympathize with al Qaeda.
- 93 percent of Muslim Americans think Muslim Americans are loyal to the United States.

Organizations to Contact

The editors have compiled the following list of organizations concerned with the issues debated in this book. The descriptions are derived from materials provided by the organizations. All have publications or information available for interested readers. The list was compiled on the date of publication of the present volume; the information provided here may change. Be aware that many organizations take several weeks or longer to respond to inquiries, so allow as much time as possible for the receipt of requested materials.

American-Arab Anti-Discrimination Committee (ADC)
4201 Connecticut Ave. NW, Ste. 300, Washington, DC 20008
(202) 244-2990
e-mail: adc@adc.org • website: www.adc.org

This organization fights anti-Arab stereotyping in the media and works to protect Arab Americans from discrimination and hate crimes. It publishes a bimonthly newsletter, the *Chronicle;* issue papers and special reports; community studies; legal, media, and educational guides; and action alerts.

AMIDEAST
1730 M St. NW, Ste. 1100, Washington, DC 20036-4505
(202) 776-9600
e-mail: inquiries@amideast.org • website: www.amideast.org

AMIDEAST supports education and development programs that promote understanding between the people of the Middle East and North Africa and Americans. It publishes several books for all age groups, including *Islam: A Primer.*

Arab-American Action Network (AAAN)
3148 W. Sixty-Third St., Chicago, IL 60629
(773) 436-6060
e-mail: info@aaan.org
website: www.aaan.org

This group strives to strengthen the Arab community by building its capacity to be an active agent for positive social change. As a grassroots nonprofit organization, its strategies include community organizing, advocacy, education, social services, leadership development, cultural outreach, and forging productive relationships with other communities.

Canadian Islamic Congress (CIC)
675 Queen St. S., Ste. 208
Kitchener, ON N2M 1A1
Canada
(519) 746-1242
website: www.cicnow.com/cic2010

The CIC seeks to establish a national Canadian network of Muslim individuals and organizations to improve the rights and welfare of Canadian Muslims. It also presents the interests of Canadian Muslims to Canadian governments, political parties, media, and other organizations. Its website contains numerous op-eds, articles, and other useful materials.

Council on American-Muslim Relations (CAIR)
453 New Jersey Ave. SE, Washington, DC 20003
(202) 488-8787 • fax: (202) 488-0833
e-mail: cair@cair-net.org • website: www.cair-net.org

CAIR is a nonprofit organization that works to defend the rights of American Muslims. It offers an Islamic perspective on public policy issues. The CAIR website features statements condemning the September 11, 2001, terrorist attacks and documents subsequent discrimination against Muslims.

International Institute of Islamic Thought (IIIT)
500 Grove St.
Herndon, VA 20170
(703) 471-1133
e-mail: iiit@iiit.org • website: www.iiit.org

The IIIT was established in 1981 as a private nonprofit academic and cultural institution dedicated to promoting research, publications, and conferences related to Islamic thought and contemporary social sciences. It publishes numerous books in both Arabic and English.

Islamic Circle of North America (ICNA)
166-26 Eighty-Ninth Ave., Jamaica, NY 11432
(718) 658-1199
e-mail: info@icna.org • website: www.icna.org

ICNA is a grassroots organization that seeks to promote Islam in all arenas of life. ICNA runs many projects, programs, charities, and activities and publishes numerous pamphlets in its *Islamic Da'wah* series as well as the monthly magazine the *Message.*

Islamic Information Center of America (IICA)
PO Box 4052
Des Plaines, IL 60016
(847) 541-8141
e-mail: iica1@comcast.net • website: www.iica.org

IICA is a nonprofit organization that provides information about Islam to Muslims, the general public, and the media. It publishes and distributes a number of pamphlets; a monthly newsletter, the *Invitation;* and books including *My Little Book About Islam, My Little Book About Allah,* and *My Little Book About the Qur'an.*

Islamic Society of North America (ISNA)
PO Box 38
Plainfield, IN 46168
(317) 839-8157
website: www.isna.net

This group seeks to encourage understanding and cooperation within the diverse Islamic community in America. The ISNA has active youth and interfaith wings.

Islamic Supreme Council of America (ISCA)
17195 Silver Pkwy. #401
Fenton, MI 48430
(810) 593-1222
website: www.islamicsupremecouncil.org

The ISCA is a religious organization that promotes Islam in America by helping American Muslims integrate Islamic teachings with American culture. The ISCA also teaches non-Muslims that Islam is a religion of moderation, peace, and tolerance. It strongly condemns Islamic extremists and all forms of terrorism. Its website includes statements, commentaries, and reports on terrorism, including *Jihad: A Misunderstood Concept from Islam* and *The Approach of Armageddon? An Islamic Perspective.*

Muslim Public Affairs Council
110 Maryland Ave. NE, Ste. 210
Washington, DC 20002
(202) 547-7701
website: www.mpac.org

The Muslim Public Affairs Council is a public service agency that advocates for the civil rights of American Muslims, for the integration of Islam into American pluralism, and for a positive, constructive relationship between American Muslims and their representatives.

Washington Institute for Near East Policy
1828 L St. NW, Washington, DC 20036
(202) 452-0650
e-mail: info@washingtoninstitute.org
website: www.washingtoninstitute.org

The institute is an independent, nonprofit research organization that provides information and analysis on the Middle East and US policy in the region. It publishes numerous books, periodic monographs, and reports on regional politics, security, and economics and hosts an entire section on Arab and Islamic politics.

Women Living Under Muslim Laws (WLUML)
International Coordination Office
PO Box 28445, London N19 5NZ
UNITED KINGDOM
e-mail: wluml@wluml.org • website: www.wluml.org

Women Living Under Muslim Laws is an international solidarity network that provides information, support, and a collective space for women whose lives are shaped, conditioned, or governed by laws and customs said to derive from Islam. For more than two decades WLUML has linked individual women and organizations. It now extends to more than seventy countries ranging from South Africa to Uzbekistan, Senegal to Indonesia, and Brazil to France.

For Further Reading

Books

Ahmed, Akbar. *Journey into America: The Challenge of Islam.* Washington, DC: Brookings Institution Press, 2010. The author, a professor of Islamic Studies at American University and a well-respected scholar of Islam, examines what it means to be Muslim in modern America.

Akyol, Mustafa. *Islam Without Extremes: A Muslim Case for Liberty.* New York: W.W. Norton, 2011. The author considers whether Islam is compatible with freedom by tracing the ideological and historical roots of political Islam.

Ali, Ayaan Hirsi. *Infidel.* New York: Free Press, 2008. The author, a Somali-born member of the Dutch parliament who faced death threats after collaborating on a film about domestic violence against Muslim women, is well-known for her outspoken criticisms of Islam. In this book, she offers a powerful feminist critique of Islam from an insider's point of view.

Armstrong, Karen. *Muhammad: A Prophet for Our Time.* New York: HarperOne, 2007. This nonfiction biography by religion expert Karen Armstrong depicts Islam's prophet as a mystic and a wise political and social reformer.

Crimp, Susan, and Joel Richardson. *Why We Left Islam: Former Muslims Speak Out.* Los Angeles: WorldNetDaily, 2008. This book contains stories of former Muslims about their decision to leave their religion.

Esposito, John L. *Islam: The Straight Path.* New York: Oxford University Press, 2010. The most recent edition of a classic Islamic studies book, this volume offers readers a sound introduction to Islam.

Esposito, John L., and Dalia Mogahed. *Who Speaks for Islam? What a Billion Muslims Really Think.* Washington, DC: Gallup, 2008. The polls and conclusions in this useful book are based on six years of research and more than fifty thousand interviews representing 1.3

billion Muslims who reside in more than thirty-five nations. This poll is the largest, most comprehensive study of its kind.

Fuller, Graham E. *A World Without Islam.* New York: Back Bay, 2011. The author, former vice chairman of the National Intelligence Council at the CIA, suggests that many of the current tensions that exist between the East and the West have geopolitical rather than religious origins and that these tensions would have arisen even in a "world without Islam."

McCarthy, Andrew C. *The Grand Jihad: How Islam and the Left Sabotage America.* New York: Encounter, 2010. This conservative author argues that the real threat to the United States is not terrorism but Islamism, which he claims has collaborated with liberals to undermine US security and threaten freedom.

Sultan, Wafa. *A God Who Hates: The Courageous Woman Who Inflamed the Muslim World Speaks Out Against the Evils of Islam.* New York: St. Martin's Griffin, 2011. This Syrian Muslim woman is well known for her outspoken criticism of Islam.

Periodicals

Ahmed, Qanta A. "In Our Silence, Muslim Americans Essentially Collaborate with the Islamists," *Christian Science Monitor,* March 29, 2011. www.csmonitor.com/Commentary/Opinion/2011/0329/In-our-silence-Muslim-Americans-essentially-collaborate-with-the-Islamists.

Ahmed, Qanta A. "Saudi Ban on Women Driving Is Against Islam," *Christian Science Monitor,* June 17, 2011. www.csmonitor.com/Commentary/Opinion/2011/0617/Saudi-ban-on-women-driving-is-against-Islam/(page)/1.

Alibhai-Brown, Yasmin. "Wearing the Burqa Is Neither Islamic nor Socially Acceptable," *Independent* (London), July 13, 2009. www.independent.co.uk/opinion/commentators/yasmin-alibhai-brown/yasmin-alibhaibrown-wearing-the-burqa-is-neither-islamic-nor-socially-acceptable-1743375.html.

Ash, Timothy Garton. "France's Burka Ban," *Los Angeles Times,* April 7, 2011. http://articles.latimes.com/2011/apr/07/opinion/la-oe-gartonash-burka-20110407.

Azwer, Maryam. "Living Beneath the Veil," *Sunday Leader* (Sri Lanka), May 22, 2011. www.thesundayleader.lk/2011/05/22/living-beneath-the-veil.

Bawer, Bruce. "An Anatomy of Surrender," *City Journal,* Spring 2008. www.city-journal.org/2008/18_2_cultural_jihadists.html.

Chowhurdy, Arshad. "A Muslim American Reflects on Osama bin Laden's Death," *Washington Post,* May 3, 2011. www.washington post.com/opinions/a-muslim-american-reflects-on-osama-bin-ladens-death/2011/05/03/AFQF7z8F_story.html.

Cline, Edward. "Islam plus Democracy Equals Islam," *Capitalism Magazine,* February 16, 2011. www.capitalismmagazine.com/war-peace/islamic-jihad/6266-islam-plus-democracy-equals-islam.html.

Esposito, John L. "Honor Killing: Is Violence Against Women a Universal Problem, Not an Islamic Issue?," *Huffington Post,* September 4, 2010. www.huffingtonpost.com/john-l-esposito/violence-against-women-a_b_705797.html.

Eteraz, Ali. "The Myth of Muslim Condemnation of Terror," *Huffington Post,* October 10, 2007. www.huffingtonpost.com/ali-eteraz/the-myth-of-muslim-condem_b_67904.html.

Gopalan, Sandeep. "Behind the Burqa," *New York Times,* January 27, 2010. www.nytimes.com/2010/01/28/opinion/28iht-edgopalan.html.

Gulen, Fethullah. "Fethullah Gulen on Islam and Democracy," FethullahGulen.com, March 4, 2011. www.fethullah-gulen.org/op-ed/fethullah-gulen-islam-democracy.html.

Hammarberg, Thomas. "Europe Must Not Ban the Burka," *Guardian* (Manchester, UK), March 8, 2010. www.guardian.co.uk/commen tisfree/2010/mar/08/europe-ban-burqa-veil.

Haussegger, Virginia. "Time to Ban the Burqa," *Age* (Australia), May 21, 2010. www.theage.com.au/opinion/society-and-culture/the-burqa-is-a-war-on-women-20100520-vnp3.html.

Haynes, Charles C. "Shariah Hysteria: Unwarranted, Unconstitutional," *GazetteXtra,* March 26, 2011. http://gazettextra.com/news/2011/mar/26/shariah-hysteria-unwarranted-unconstitutional.

Hopida, Edgar. "For Muslims in U.S., a Sense of Relief," *San Diego Union-Tribune,* May 3, 2011. www.signonsandiego.com /news/2011/may/03/for-muslims-in-us-a-sense-of-relief.

Imani, Amil. "Dear Rep. King: Forget 'Radical'—Islam Is the Culprit," *American Thinker,* March 10, 2011. www.american thinker.com/2011/03/dear_rep_king_forget_radical_i.html.

Khan, Sheema. "In the Struggle for Islam's Soul, Silence Is Not an Option," *Globe & Mail* (Toronto), January 12, 2011.

Kristof, Nicholas D. "Is Islam the Problem?," *New York Times,* March 6, 2011.

Kuligowski, Monte. "Should the U.S. Surrender Freedom to Stop Islamic Terror?," RenewAmerica.com, April 12, 2011. www .renewamerica.com/columns/kuligowski/110412.

Malik, Mustafa. "Muslim Terrorism in America Can't Be Combated Without Addressing Its Source," *New Statesman,* March 19, 2011. www.statesman.com/opinion/malik-muslim-terrorism-in-america -cant-be- combated-1333680.html.

Marin, Minette. "It's Not a Phobia, Lady Warsi—It's Rational to Fear Islam," *Sunday Times* (London), January 23, 2011.

Massie, Mychal. "Islam Slips the Noose Again," WorldNetDaily .com, March 22, 2011. www.wnd.com/index.php?fa=PAGE .view&pageId=277773.

Mirahmadi, Hcdich, and Mehreen Farooq. "After Osama bin Laden's Death, Time for a New Poster Child for Islam," *Christian Science Monitor,* May 3, 2011. http://www.csmonitor.com/Commentary /Opinion/2011/0503/After-Osama-bin-Laden-s-death-time-for-a new-poster-child-for-Islam.

Peters, Ralph. "Fort Hood's 9/11," *New York Post,* November 6, 2009. www.nypost.com/p/news/opinion/opedcolumnists/item_xjP9y GrJN7gI7zdsJ31vnJ.

Pipes, Daniel. "Major Hasan's Islamist Life," *FrontPage Magazine,* November 20, 2009. http://frontpagemag.com/2009/ll/20/major -hasan's-islamist-life---by-daniel-pipes.

Rana, Bilal. "Real Muslim Leadership, Not a Terrorist's Death, Would Be Something to Celebrate," *Baltimore Sun,* May 5, 2011.

www.baltimoresun.com/news/opinion/oped/bs-ed-muslims
-20110505,0,2395008.story.

Sahloul, Zaher. "Saving Our State or Destroying Our Democracy?,"
Council of Islamic Organizations of Greater Chicago, December
1, 2010. www.ciogc.org/Go.aspx?link=7655363.

Saudi Gazette, "Does Islam Oppress Women?," March 11, 2011.
www.saudigazette.com.sa/index.cfm?method-home.regcon
&contentID=2011031195594.

Al-Sheha, Abdur-Rahman Abdul-Kareem. "Islam is the Religion of
Peace," IslamLand.com, December 24, 2009. http://www.islam
land.com/EN/Contents.aspx?AID=78.

Siddiqui, Haroon. "Not Much Islamic About Islamic Pakistan,"
Toronto Star, March 6, 2011. http://www.thestar.com/opinion
/editorialopinion/article/949250--siddiqui-not-much-islamic
-about-islamic-pakistan.

Siddiqui, Haroon. "Poking Muslims in the Eye," *Toronto Star,*
April 7, 2011. http://www.thestar.com/opinion/editorialopinion
/article/970485--siddiqui-poking-muslims-in-the-eye.

Stillwell, Cinnamon. "Honor Killings: When the Ancient and the
Modern Collide," *San Francisco Chronicle,* January 23, 2008. www
.sfgate.com/cgi-bin/article.cgi?file=/g/a/2008/01/23/cstillwell
.DTL.

Suaedy, Ahmad. "Islam, Democracy, and the 2009 Elections,"
Jakarta Post (Indonesia), April 21, 2009. www.thejakartapost.com
/news/2009/04/21/islam-democracy-and-2009-elections.html.

Syed, Aijaz Zaka. "No Time to Hide for Muslims," *Khaleej Times*
(Dubai, UAE), November 30, 2008. www.khaleejtimes.com
/DisplayArticleNew.asp?col=?ion=opinion&xfile=data/opinion
/2008/November/opinion November122.xml.

Tayeh, Rayeed N. "I'm Sorry You Are Scared of Me; My Religion
Shouldn't Frighten You," *Salt Lake City Deseret News,* October
29, 2010. www.deseretnews.com/article/700077154/Im-sorry-you
-are-scared-of-me-my-religion-shouldnt-frighten-you.html.

Testriono, "Indonesia Proves That Islam Is Compatible with
Democracy," *Daily Star* (Beirut, Lebanon), April 15, 2011, p. 7.

www.dailystar.com.lb/Apr/15/Indonesia- proves-that-Islam-is -compatible-with-democracy.ashx#axzz1OFet2t5d.

Windle, Jeanette. "Is Democracy Enough?," January 10, 2009. http://jeanettewindle.blogspot.com/2009/01/is-democracy-enough .html.

Wittman, George H. "Democracy and Islam," *American Spectator,* March 23, 2011. http://spectator.org/archives/2011/03/23/democ racy-and-islam#.

Yasin, Rahil. "Are Islam and Democracy Compatible?," CounterCurrents.org, March 21, 2009. www.countercurrents.org /yasin210309.htm.

Websites

Al-Islam.org (www.al-islam.org/). This extensive website promotes Islam via informative articles that discuss the basic tenets and practices of the religion.

Free Muslims Coalition (www.freemuslims.org/). This site is run by Muslims who oppose terrorism and extremism. Formed in the wake of the September 11, 2001, attacks, the group seeks to eliminate Islamic extremism and terrorism and to strengthen secular democratic institutions in the Middle East and the Muslim world by supporting Islamic reformation efforts.

Islam-Watch (http://islam-watch.org). This site, run by former Muslims, is heavily critical of Islam, pointing out inconsistencies in the Koran. It features articles by widely published critics of Islam, such as Amil Imani and Ayaan Hirsi Ali.

Islamist-Watch (www.islamist-watch.org). This site is a project of the Middle East Forum. It combats the ideas and institutions of lawful Islamism in the United States and throughout the West. It argues that moderate Islam is the solution to radical Islam and hosts numerous articles and posts on this subject.

Jihad Watch (www.jihadwatch.org). This site, run by conservative Robert Spencer, chronicles jihadist activities with blog entries, news updates, and in-depth articles.

The Koran (http://quod.lib.umich.edu/k/koran/). This electronic edition of the Muslim holy book, translated by M.H. Shakir and published by Tahrike Tarsile (Qur'an, Inc.), is housed by the University of Michigan. Users can search the text by word or phrase, or browse it chapter by chapter.

Latino American Dawah Organization (LADO) (www.latinod awah.org). This organization promotes Islam among the American Latino community. In addition to teaching about Islam, it discusses the legacy of Islam in Spain and Latin America and focuses on Latino-Muslim relations in the United States.

U.S.-Muslim Engagement Project (www.usmuslimengagement .org). This site is sponsored by three nongovernmental, non-profit, US-based organizations: the Consensus Building Institute, Convergence, and the Institute for Resource and Security. It promotes cross-societal dialogue among public and private thought leaders, opinion leaders, and decision makers from the United States and Muslim societies.

Index

on treatment of Muslims living in US, *109*

on US mosques and violence, 34

T

Taliban, 41, 55, 71

Tamil Tigers, 22

Terrorism
  is politically motivated, 22
  plots thwarted by American Muslim cooperation, 26
  See also Islamic terrorism

Time (magazine), 55, 99, 101

Triangle Center on Terrorism and Homeland Security, 26

Turkey, secularism in, 8

U

Udas, Ayman, 55

Umar (successor to Muhammad), 15

United Nations Population Fund, 78

United States
  is right to link Muslims with terrorists, 32–37
  Islamic law threatens, 104–110
  Islamic terrorism is inspired by policies of, 38–43
  loyalty among Muslim Americans to, 9, 28
  Muslim population in, 114
  numbers of mosques in, 100–101

policies are not the reason for Islamic terrorism, 44–50

threat of sharia to, is irrational, 111–116

unfairly links Muslims with terrorists, 25–31

V

The veil
  bans on, 66
  does not necessarily oppress women, 70–75
  oppresses women, 65–69
  whole face, *68*

W

WikiLeaks, 41

Windle, Jeanette, 8

Wolf, Naomi, 70

Women
  Islam condones honor killings of, 76–82
  Islam grants rights to, 58–64
  Islam oppresses, 52–57
  Koran on punishment for sexual offenses by, 81
  sharia and, 8–9
  the veil does not necessarily oppress, 70–75
  the veil oppresses, 65–69

Women's rights
  Muslim nations ranking lowest on, *54*
  Koran on, *63*

World Economic Forum, 54

Picture Credits

AP Images/Bell County Sheriff's Department, 15

AP Images/David Duprey, 86

AP Images/Killeen Daily Herald, David Morris, 36

AP Images/K.M. Chaudary, 80

AP Images/Mary Altaffer, 113

AP Images/M. Spencer Green, 100

AP Images/The Orange County Register, Mindy Schauer, 89

AP Images/Osama Faisel, 56

AP Images/Swoan Parker, 95

© CulturalEyes-AusGS/Alamy, 11

Gale/Cengage Learning, 17, 21, 29, 35, 54, 63, 68, 79, 85, 92, 102, 109, 115

Jin Lee/Bloomberg via Getty Images, 23

© Jenny Matthews/Alamy, 67, 72

Mujahed Mohammed/AFP/Getty Images, 60

Michael Reynolds/EPA/Landov, 27

Reuters/Landov, 48

© Alex Segre/Alamy, 106

Shirley Shepard/AFP/Getty Images, 42

© Rob Walls/Alamy, 51